Trail and Fell Running

in the
Yorkshire Dales

**40 runs
in the National Park,
including the Three Peaks**

by Pete Ellwood

CICERONE

Juniper House, Murley Moss,
Oxenholme Road, Kendal, Cumbria LA9 7RL

www.cicerone.co.uk

© Pete Ellwood 2019

First edition 2019

ISBN: 978 1 85284 922 1

Printed by KHL Printing, Singapore

A catalogue record for this book is available from the British Library.

© Crown copyright 2019
OS PU100012932

All photographs are by the author unless otherwise stated.

Updates to this guide

While every effort is made by our authors to ensure the accuracy of guidebooks as they go to print, changes can occur during the lifetime of an edition. Any updates that we know of for this guide will be on the Cicerone website (www.cicerone.co.uk/922/updates), so please check before planning your trip. We also advise that you check information about such things as transport, accommodation and shops, locally. Even rights of way can be altered over time. We are always grateful for information about any discrepancies between a guidebook and the facts on the ground, sent by email to updates@cicerone.co.uk or by post to

Cicerone,
Juniper House,
Murley Moss,
Oxenholme Road,
Kendal, LA9 7RL.

Register your book: To sign up to receive free updates, special offers and GPX files where available, register your book at www.cicerone.co.uk.

Acknowledgements

This book would not have been possible without the help and support of a large number of people. I would like to take this opportunity to thank all the Settle Harriers who checked routes and posed for, or provided, photographs. Thanks also to Andrew Hinde and Rae Lonsdale for their help with the introduction and mountain rescue sections, and to Lee and Glyn, my long-time running partners, for keeping me out in the hills over many years. Special thanks to Adrian Dellbridge and Andy Ward for taking many of the photographs and for trying to make me look like the runner I am in my mind's eye and to OMM and Helly Hansen for providing equipment.

Huge thanks to the Cicerone team, Jonathan, Joe, Andrea, Sian and Verity, for their support in turning a vague idea into an actual book.

Most of all I would like to thank my wife, Alice, and the boys, Charlie and Harry, without whose love and support this book wouldn't have been written. For their patience and understanding of my need to be outside in the hills as often as possible, thank you.

Front cover: Superb grassy running along one of the magnificent Howgill ridges (Route 16)

Contents

Looking accross the clouds from Whernside to Ingleborough (Route 11)

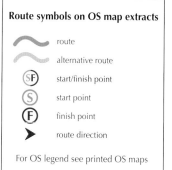

Route symbols on OS map extracts

~ route

~ alternative route

(SF) start/finish point

(S) start point

(F) finish point

➤ route direction

For OS legend see printed OS maps

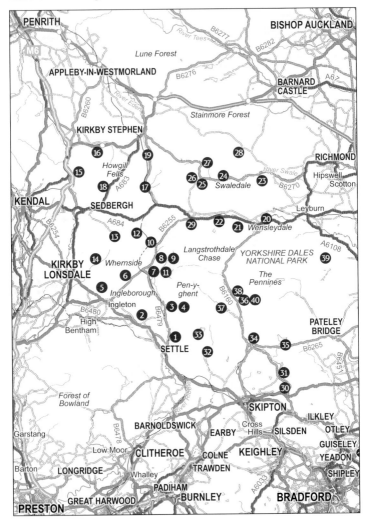

Route summary table

No.	Name	Start	Grid Reference	Distance	Ascent	Grade	Time	Page
1	Settle Loop	Settle	SD 830 652	13km (8 miles)	440m (1440ft)	2	2hr	36
2	Crummackdale	Austwick	SD 769 691	12km (7½ miles)	325m (1070ft)	3	2hr	40
3	Pen-y-ghent	Horton in Ribblesdale	SD 807 725	11km (7 miles)	560m (1840ft)	2	2hr	44
4	The Three Peaks	Horton in Ribblesdale	SD 807 725	40km (24¾ miles)	1610m (5280ft)	3	6hr	48
5	Gragareth	Ingleton	SD 691 756	11.5km (7 miles)	390m (1280ft)	4	2hr	57
6	Ingleborough (from Hill Inn)	Chapel-le-Dale	SD 745 777	8.5km (5¼ miles)	445m (1460ft)	5	1hr 30min	61
7	Ingleborough (via Park Fell)	Ribblehead	SD 765 792	14km (8¾ miles)	545m (1790ft)	3	2hr	65
8	Dodd Fell	Ribblehead	SD 782 802	19.5km (12 miles)	470m (1540ft)	4	3hr	69
9	Cosh	Ribblehead	SD 782 802	27.5km (17 miles)	745m (2450ft)	5	4hr	74
10	Great Knoutberry	Stonehouse	SD 790 834	11.6km (7 miles)	525m (1720ft)	4	2hr	80

No.	Name	Start	Grid Reference	Distance	Ascent	Grade	Time	Page
11	Whernside (from Ribblehead)	Ribblehead	SD 765 792	13km (8 miles)	715m (2350ft)	3	2hr	84
12	Dent to Ribblehead	Dent	SD 763 875	14.5km (9 miles)	500m (1640ft)	2	2hr	88
13	Whernside (from Dent)	Dent	SD 703 871	19.5km (12 miles)	655m (2150ft)	3	3hr	93
14	Barbondale	Barbon	SD 656 828	16.5km (10¼ miles)	950m (3120ft)	5	3hr	97
15	Black Force (Howgills)	Sedbergh	SD 624 995	9.5km (6 miles)	555m (1820ft)	5	1hr 30min	102
16	Bowderdale	Ravenstonedale	NY 683 050	20km (12½ miles)	1110m (3640ft)	5	3hr 30min	106
17	Wild Boar Fell	Garsdale Head	SD 777 963	16.5km (10¼ miles)	640m (2100ft)	4	2hr 30min	112
18	Cautley Spout	Sedbergh	SD 698 969	17km (10½ miles)	1110m (3640ft)	4	3hr	116
19	Pendragon Castle to Skipton Castle Ultra Leg 1 (Pendragon Castle to Hawes)	Kirkby Stephen	NY 781 025	21.5km (13½ miles)	415m (1360ft)	1	3hr	120
20	Asygarth	Aysgarth	SE 011 887	18km (11¼ miles)	315m (1030ft)	1	2hr 30min	127

No.	Name	Start	Grid Reference	Distance	Ascent	Grade	Time	Page
21	Thornton Rust	Thornton Rust	SD 972 888	15km (9½ miles)	410m (1350ft)	2	2hr	132
22	Bainbridge	Bainbridge	SD 933 901	22.5km (14 miles)	840m (2760ft)	3	3hr 30min	136
23	Maiden Castle (Reeth)	Reeth	SE 020 982	18.5km (11½ miles)	740m (2430ft)	2	2hr 30min	141
24	Gunnerside Gill	Gunnerside	SD 950 982	15km (9¼ miles)	575m (1890ft)	4	2hr 30min	146
25	Muker	Muker	SD 910 978	9km (5½ miles)	400m (1310ft)	3	1hr 30min	150
26	Great Shunner Fell	Thwaite	SD 889 983	13km (8 miles)	630m (2070ft)	2	2hr	154
27	Tan Hill (from Keld)	Keld	NY 893 012	17.5km (10¾ miles)	540m (1770ft)	4	2hr 30min	158
28	Arkengarthdale	Whaw	NY 981 042	26.5km (16½ miles)	540m (1770ft)	5	3hr 30min	163
29	Pendragon Cast e to Skipton Castle Ultra Leg 2 (Hawes to Kettlewell)	Hawes	SD 867 897	33km (20 miles)	1115m (3660ft)	2	4hr 30min	169
30	Bolton Abbey	Bolton Abbey	SE 071 539	12km (7½ miles)	220m (720ft)	2	1hr 30min	177

No.	Name	Start	Grid Reference	Distance	Ascent	Grade	Time	Page
31	Simon's Seat	Bolton Abbey	SE 052 574	13.5km (11 miles)	460m (1510ft)	2	2hr	181
32	Malham Cove and Gordale Scar	Malham	SD 900 627	11.5km (7 miles)	220m (720ft)	3	1hr 30min	185
33	Mastiles Lane	Malham	SD 894 658	25.5km (16 miles)	640m (2100ft)	1	3hr 30min	189
34	Grass Wood and Conistone Dib	Grassington	SE 002 636	13km (8 miles)	320m (1050ft)	1	2hr	194
35	Trollers Gill	Grassington	SE 063 639	17km (10½ miles)	385m (1260ft)	3	2hr 30min	198
36	Great Whernside (from Kettlewell)	Kettlewell	SD 968 723	12.5km (7¾ miles)	595m (1950ft)	3	2hr	203
37	Fountains Fell	Arncliffe	SD 930 719	25.5km (16 miles)	630m (2070ft)	2	3hr 30min	207
38	Buckden Pike	Starbotton	SD 953 746	13km(8 miles)	555m (1820ft)	3	2hr	214
39	Masham Moor	Masham	SE 153 809	19.5km(12 miles)	525m (1720ft)	4	3hr	218
40	Pendragon Castle to Skipton Castle Ultra Leg 3 (Kettlewell to Skipton)	Kettlewell	SD 968 723	30.5km(19 miles)	730m (2400ft)	2	4hr 30min	223

Descending the grassy slopes of Arant Haw (Route 18)

Good running on the Pennine Bridleway descent from Dodd Fell (Route 8) (photo: Andy Ward)

Introduction

Running is one of the most popular sports in the world, which is a reflection of its inherent simplicity and ease of participation. Running in the hills and mountains can provide us with some of our best running experiences. The benefits, motivations and incentives of running, of which there are many, include the following:

Enjoyment

Being out in the countryside in the fresh air, enjoying gorgeous views and having memorable experiences, provides an escape from the more mundane aspects of the day job and family life, and allows runners a moment to themselves, for their own enjoyment and wellbeing.

Fitness

Running burns calories, makes the lungs and heart stronger and releases chemical endorphins that provide the feel-good factor. Plenty of good research demonstrates the positive health benefits of regular exercise. Running on paths and tracks reduces the repetitive stresses and strains on the body compared with running on roads. Each footstep is planted differently; your eyes and brain must coordinate their responses to negotiate the terrain ahead. Running also strengthens mental resilience and can clear the mind, allowing you to focus on the challenges ahead. When the weather takes a turn for the worse, the mental toughness needed to complete a long day out in the hills is immense.

Competition

Fell running offers different types of races: big and small, short or long, take your pick. Other events include challenges where completion is the name of the game.

Fell racing is an excellent way to discover the Dales, and the variety of races available mean that you can race for just a couple of miles or for over

The long descent from Great Coum to Barbondale (Route 14)

Welcome to the Yorkshire Dales

twenty. Fell racing provides a different type of enjoyment and challenge and is the culmination of weeks, sometimes months, of training. Turning up on the start line with similar-minded people, all with their own version of the 'no I am not fit at the moment' comment or a description of a niggly injury is not uncommon. Inevitably, they will speed away from you as race begins. Most runners can usually manage a good final sprint, and the shared sense of achievement as you cross the finish line is tremendous. A shake of the hand with your fellow competitors is usually followed by a discussion of how hard it was and which sections you ran well.

Containing some of the finest running terrain in the British Isles, the Yorkshire Dales covers an area of over 2000km^2 in northern England,

sandwiched between the Lake District and the Pennines. The abundance of good paths and tracks make running in the Dales an amazing experience, and one that is accessible to most of us, with a mixture of medium-sized peaks and broad open moorlands to climb and run across. This book contains what I consider to be forty of the best routes in the Dales, including runs up the iconic mountains of Whernside, Ingleborough and Pen-y-ghent, as well as routes that traverse the moors in the far north of the region. From the honeypot sites of Malham and Grassington, to runs in the Howgills (the Yorkshire Dales National Park boundary was extended in August 2016 to include the northern Howgills, among other areas), there is a route in this book to suit runners of differing abilities.

THE YORKSHIRE DALES

History and geology

The word 'dale' comes from the ancient Norse word 'dalr' meaning valley. The Yorkshire Dales National Park (YDNP) covers over 800 square miles of these valleys, taking in a section of the central Pennines from Skipton and Settle in the south to Sedbergh and Reeth in the north.

Some dales, such as the Swale, Ure, Nidd and Wharfe, flow east and empty into the North Sea, while others, such as the Ribble, Lune and Eden, flow west to the Irish Sea.

The Dales rise in areas of high gritstone moorland or mountains, with the majority cutting through deep bands of limestone created 300 million years ago from the remains of marine crustaceans that lived in shallow tropical seas; the Dales at that time was positioned south of the equator. The rocks contain rich veins of minerals and metals that were mined for centuries, bringing wealth and employment to the area.

The last ice age changed the landscape into the one we are familiar with today. Classic features such as u-shaped valleys abound, each filled with a river too small to ever have formed it. There are also characteristic features such as Malham Cove, a 300ft-high dry cove, which incredibly became a waterfall for the first time in two centuries during Storm Desmond in December 2015.

Overlying the natural geology and geomorphology of the area is the influence of mankind over the past two thousand years. There

Swaledale, a typical glaciated valley

Remains of the old lead mines at Gunnerside Gill (Route 24)

are few places in the Dales that are untouched by human activity, the whole area being criss-crossed by drystone walls, roads, railway lines and settlements.

Since prehistoric times, through to later Roman and Monastic periods, people have moved through the Dales developing a system of paths and tracks that are still used today, albeit for different purposes. Drove routes established in the sixteenth and seventeenth centuries created trails for transporting cattle and lead from the mines throughout the area, many of which are still in use today. Swaledale also has an ancient corpse road, along which the bodies of the dead were carried to a church for burial in consecrated ground.

The Romans were among the first to develop a network of roads, linking forts and towns to aid the movement of troops as they sought to subdue the native tribes. Later, these were used to access and exploit mineral resources from the region.

During the middle ages, the great monasteries of Bolton, Rievaulx and Fountains owned vast areas of land in the Dales, which they used for sheep farming, while they also continued to build up profitable mining businesses, extracting metals (mainly lead) from deep underground.

Upland farming is a common feature in the Dales, with relatively small farms keeping flocks of sheep and small herds of cattle. This has created the flower-rich hay meadow habitats of the Dales today. Traditionally, the hay was stored in stone barns that were once common across the Dales; it was kept in lofts above the byres that housed the cattle.

Most recently the Dales has become a popular tourist destination. People are drawn by the beautiful scenery and wide open spaces or are seeking the challenge of the many outdoor pursuits available in the area. TV programmes such as James Herriot's *All Creatures Great and Small* and iconic events such as the Tour De France have all showcased the area.

Nesting restrictions

Most of the runs involve areas of high moorland or mountains. In the spring, these come alive with the sound of

Meadow pipit

returning birds, such as the curlew, lapwing and golden plover. However, the numbers of these birds have decreased in recent years and for that reason restrictions have been introduced in some areas; between March and July runners with dogs are asked to keep them on a lead to minimise the disturbance to ground-nesting birds. Spring is also lambing time, and runners are asked to keep their dogs under close control around sheep at this time. Many grouse moors may be closed in the early autumn. For up-to-date access details visit www.yorkshiredales.org.uk.

Accommodation

The Dales contains sufficient accommodation for all tastes and budgets; camp sites, youth hostels, pubs, B&Bs, self-catering cottages and hotels are present in all the major population centres and Dales. For further details visit www.yorkshire.com and www.yorkshiredales.org.uk.

Transport

Transport in the Dales is predominantly by road. The area is bordered by the M6 to the west, the A1 and A1M to the east, the A65 and A59 to the south and the A66 to the north. The A684 crosses the middle of the Dales from west to east. Minor roads pass through all the individual dales, and there are many smaller roads crossing from one dale to another.

Various public transport options are available from the main towns

Steam train on the Settle – Carlisle line (Route 19)

into the Dales. The main bus service is the Dales Bus (www.dalesbus.org). The Rail to Trail service uses the Bentham line, which runs between Morecombe and Leeds, to access the southern Dales (www.communityrail lancashire.co.uk). Additionally, there are a growing number of community bus links operating, including The Little White Bus (www.littlewhitebus.co.uk), which serves the Upper Dales; the Northern Dalesman Bus (www.dalesbus.org/northerndalesman), which covers an area from Ribblehead through Wensleydale and Swaledale to Richmond; and the Western Dales Bus (www.westerndalesbus.co.uk), which runs between Dent and the Howgills. Many of these services are seasonal and run less frequently during the winter months.

Details of public transport links are outlined in each route description. Railway access to the Dales is mainly via the Settle–Carlisle line (www.settle-carlisle.co.uk), which runs from Skipton, through Settle to Dent and Kirkby Stephen. The line offers much in the way of linear routes, allowing the runner to travel to different parts of the Dales before running back over the hills to the start of the route. Many of the routes in the south-west Dales and Three Peaks section can be run from this line.

Maps

OS maps of the Yorkshire Dales are printed in two scales: 1:50,000 and 1:25,000. The detail provided by the larger scale map is useful in poor weather conditions and if you are unfamiliar with the area. Harvey's also produce maps of the Dales in two scales: 1:40,000 and 1:25,000.

Maps are available from the many outdoor equipment shops in the Dales and online. They are also available as downloads from the Ordnance Survey (OS) and other apps, such as ViewRanger. However, when using maps on a phone or mobile device it is imperative that you are aware of battery life and signal strength in remote areas. Runners need to be able to navigate accurately using whichever maps they choose.

RUNNING IN THE YORKSHIRE DALES

A brief history

Running is a relatively old sport in the region, with Burnsall being the oldest recorded fell race in the Dales, dating back to 1882. Many of the agricultural shows, large and small, would feature a race to the summit of a local fell, where locals competed against each other for the prize of returning first to the show field. Fell races sat comfortably with other local competitions, such as dry-stone walling, horse jumping, stick dressing and the showing of livestock, especially sheep, against a backdrop of a largely agricultural economy where betting was a large part of the event. Over the years, many of the greatest fell runners of their generation, including Ernest Dalzell, Bill Teasdale, Fred Reeves and Tommy Sedgwick, competed in these races. They brought an air of eager anticipation to the late afternoon, as the front runners ascended the fell at great speed before descending, even faster, steep and sometimes rocky escarpments to finally sprint across the show field to rapturous cheers and applause. Fred Reeve's 1977 Burnsall record of 12min 47s still stands. Many of these races are still run today, organised by either the show committee, BOFRA (British Open Fell Runners Association) or the FRA (Fell Running Association). Other races have also taken place for many years, including

Runners competing in the Pen-y-ghent race

the Fellsman Hike, which originated in 1962. Organised by the Keighley Scout Service Group, this linear route starts from Ingleton and traverses the Dales, with the winners finishing the 61 miles in Grassington, just over ten hours later.

Tracks and trails

Trail running has recently become a popular addition to our sport, and the Dales provides an extensive network of paths, bridleways, tracks, trails and roads, offering some of the finest fell and trail running. Many of these routes follow ancient drove roads that were once used for transporting vital supplies between one dale and another. The rise in popularity of trail running has led to an increase in organised events covering a range of distances, from 10km to over 50km; many of which are low-key, non-competitive events. Participants navigate the course using a map and a written route description, via well-stocked checkpoints, to the finish.

In recent years walking, mountain biking and running for leisure have grown enormously, with many more people taking up the sport of running and visiting the Yorkshire Dales to pursue their hobby. The popular tourist centres of Settle, Sedbergh, Hawes and Reeth cater for outdoor sports and increasingly for runners, with shops and guiding services readily available.

Crossing the Dales are several long distance trails; the most well

Signpost: 'Hawes'

known of which are the Pennine Way and the Dales Way. The Pennine Way runs from Edale in the Peak District to Kirk Yetholm in the Scottish borders. The Spine Race, which is held each January, runs the length of the Pennine Way, the completion of which is a fantastic achievement. The Dales Way, which runs through the Dales, traverses Wharfedale from Ilkley before crossing the Cam High Road into Dentdale, finishing at a point overlooking Lake Windermere at Bowness. At 81 miles, this route makes a good multi-day running (otherwise known as 'fastpacking') trip.

Three Peaks race

The most famous long race in the Dales is the Three Peaks Race. Held annually in April, the race comprises the Yorkshire Three Peaks of Pen-y-ghent, Whernside and Ingleborough, starting and finishing in Horton in Ribblesdale. In common with most races, the winners complete the course in superhuman times. The current women's record stands at 3hr 9min (Victoria Wilkinson, 2017), while the men's record is 2hr 46min (Andy Peace, 1996). The mid-pack usually takes between four to five hours to reach the finish. Route 4 in the South-West Dales and Three Peaks section of this book describes a route that takes in these three famous peaks. Be aware it does not describe the classic Three Peaks race route. Sometimes criticised as more of a trail race by fell runners, the Three Peaks Race is a hard route with fast running on good tracks, many of which have recently been improved, between each of the peaks. The final run-off, from the summit of Ingleborough, seems much

The badge of the Three Peaks Club (Image trademark of the 'Three Peaks Cafe')

longer than normal, even though from early on the finish marquee can be seen in the distance. The final run-in, across the field, under the railway, around someone's garden, across the road and over the final few metres of grass, is accompanied by cheers from the large crowd and the announcement of your name over the tannoy system. This is markedly different to

The author representing Settle Harriers in the FRA Relays Kettlewell (photo: Alex Pilkington)

other fell races. As a local runner, the support you receive throughout the race is unbelievable and well worth all the hard miles of training.

Other events

The Yorkshire Dales offers a wide range of different races, from the short and fast races at Burnsall and Kilnsey Shows to the longer classic events like the Three Peaks Race. Equally, many challenge events are held in the Dales each year, often raising money for charities, such as mountain rescue teams, allowing them to continue their superb work.

For details of other races and events, visit the following websites: FRA (www.fellrunner.uk.org), BOFRA (www.bofra.org.uk), the Trail Running Association (TRA) (www.tra-uk.org) or YDNP (www.yorkshiredales.org.uk).

Running clubs

The Dales offers many well-attended running clubs. Most of the larger towns have a club that trains on the fells, and they are always open to new members and visitors. For further details visit www.fellrunner.uk.org.

Equipment

Running, at its heart, is about a pair of trainers, a pair of shorts and a t-shirt. This simplicity is what many runners crave and partly why many of us choose to run.

The weather, the time of year and the length and difficulty of the route often make this simple approach more complex. A runner's equipment and clothing are a personal choice that reflects experience, ability and general mindset. Suggestions of what to wear or carry (depending on the weather) in summer conditions

A selection of winter running kit

A selection of trainers showing the type of grip needed

include the following: a waterproof/ windproof top; fell or trail-running shoes; long or short-sleeved base layer; shorts; socks; buff or hat; gloves; whistle; simple first aid kit; food; a map of the area; a compass; and, of course, the ability to use the last two.

Consideration should also be given to the weather conditions on the day. Always bear in mind that the weather on the top of the mountain can be much windier and colder than in the valley bottom. A long-sleeved top and bottoms should be worn or carried, just in case.

A route that can be run in shorts and a short sleeved base layer (with a windproof just in case) in summer can be completely different in winter, when the weather conditions can be much more difficult and the visibility much poorer.

Extra winter kit could include spare clothing, thicker base layers, hats and gloves, extra food, a head torch, a survival bag and possibly micro crampons and running poles. These days, a fully charged mobile phone is a useful piece of additional kit; although this should never replace a map due to unreliable mobile coverage and limited battery life.

And finally, footwear. Everyone has their favourite running shoe. Again, your choice of shoe depends on the route, the weather conditions and, of course, personal preference. A good pair of trail or fell shoes with substantial grip should be enough for the routes in this book, most of which are on paths and tracks. All good outdoor shops should be able to advise as to which shoe type is best for different terrains.

Navigation

The ability to use a map and compass is essential. There are a multitude of courses, books and websites that can teach you how to navigate safely and effectively. The most important aspect is to be able to understand the information provided by the map and relate it to what you see around you; this allows you to accurately fix your position.

How you choose to navigate is a personal choice. The rise in popularity of digital mapping and navigation apps on smartphones has led to runners taking a mixed approach to navigation. When researching the runs in this book, I always carried a physical map and compass, having been brought up in the days before such technology was invented. At the same time, I would record the run on a GPS watch while running a navigation app on my phone. I found this combination to be the most useful.

Runners should carry an appropriate map, in a waterproof bag, and be able to use it to navigate each route. Many of us choose to carry a phone to record our runs. While phones have improved over the past few years, batteries are not guaranteed to last when running GPS navigation apps, and especially in cold conditions. In addition, they should always be carried in a waterproof pouch.

When reccying the routes, the single most useful piece of navigational equipment was a print out of a digital map, with the route highlighted, which was placed in a polypocket or map case to prevent it from getting wet and the ink running. This was always in my hand. It was easy to fold up into something small enough to carry, and it did not matter if it got a bit scrunched or dirty. Having it at hand meant I often referred to it, unlike the full-scale map in my rucksack, which seldom came out. Frequent referencing meant I was quicker to notice if I went off route, reducing the chance of getting lost.

Safety and mountain rescue

A runner is responsible for their own safety as they move through the mountains. There are a few precautions that should always be taken to minimise the chance of a small slip or slight navigational error escalating into a larger incident.

First, always carry the appropriate level of kit for the run. It is also important to recognise when you should put on that waterproof jacket or hat and gloves. Many runners on longer runs find that they can keep going the extra distance, while all the time their bodies may be cooling down if the weather conditions are poor. Runners need to be aware of the causes and effects of hypothermia and how to prevent it.

Running regularly inevitably means you are likely to have a small slip or take a tumble at some point. How you respond to these incidents is important in preventing the situation

Maps and navigation aids: a map in a polypocket is simple and effective

getting worse. To begin with, check you are ok to carry on. Do you need to take a shorter route back to the start? Consider walking for a few minutes to give your body time to settle down; or, if need be, walk all the way back. Consider putting on extra clothing. If the injury is serious and you cannot continue, then consider calling mountain rescue. Call 999, ask for the police and inform them that you need mountain rescue. They will ask you to provide some basic information: current location – preferably a description with place names and a six-figure grid reference; the nature of the injury; and your details. Although phone coverage in the Dales has improved over the years, you are not guaranteed to get a good signal. If your phone reads 'emergency calls only', your 999 call will 'roam' to another network, enabling you to reach the Police; however, please be aware that no one will be able to ring you back. In this situation call 999 again ten minutes later, so that someone with local area knowledge may be able to clarify your initial information. Also consider sending a text message (which is more likely to work than a voice call) to someone who is able to help.

Remember, mountain rescue teams are staffed by unpaid volunteers who will leave their jobs and families to respond to a call-out. Always consider whether you really need their help. If your smartphone signal is strong enough to send data, a mountain rescue team can use the SARLOC system to pinpoint your location if you follow their texted instructions. Runners can register their phones with www.emergencysms.org.uk, which allows text messages to be sent and received in areas where mobile phone network coverage is poor. If you have an accident and cannot move, blow your whistle six times in succession each minute; this is the internationally recognised distress call for requesting help.

All the above becomes more important if running solo. Before setting out on a run, a sensible precaution would be to leave a route description and estimated finish time with someone, with instructions on what to do if you are not back, or in contact, by a certain time. But make sure you remember call them to say you're safe.

The weather can affect run times and conditions considerably. Accurate weather forecasts are available from many sources. A good starting point would be either the Mountain Weather Information Service (www.mwis.org.uk) or the Met Office (www.metoffice.gov.uk). The weather in the mountains can be much more severe than many runners from outside the area are used to. Combined with the minimalistic nature of running clothing, it can potentially have a greater impact on runners than walkers. Always carry additional clothing and be prepared to modify your route if weather conditions change for the worse.

Cattle, not usually high on any safety list, can occasionally cause problems in the Dales, generally in early spring when bullocks are let out of their winter barns on to the spring pastures. These giddy beasts can stampede, and cows with calves may pose a greater risk if they feel their calves are threatened. Consider using an alternative route to avoid them. This potential threat is much more pronounced when running with a dog. Dogs should be kept on a short lead, and if the cows approach aggressively, let go of the lead, as the cattle see the dog as a threat. The cows will chase the dog, which can out run them; runners probably not.

Using this guide

The forty runs follow an arc from Skipton in the south through the southern Dales, ending at Arkengarthdale in the northern Dales. Most runs are a mixture of trail and fell, with a few runs being solely one or the other. The runs are split into four areas.

The south-west Dales and Three Peaks

This area is typically mountainous, with some of the mountains being quite rocky. The hills are criss-crossed by a good network of footpaths, tracks and bridleways. Being the most popular area of the Dales, it caters to a wide range of outdoor sports, including running, caving, paragliding, mountain biking and cycling, as well as to

Giddy cattle

Outstanding running in the Howgills (Route 15)

tourists who visit the area for the scenery. The area is served by the popular towns and villages of Settle, Horton in Ribblesdale and Ingleton.

The north-west Dales and Howgills

This area is also mountainous, but the mountains are grassier and rounder in nature, while the Howgills are noted for their steepness. It has a more remote atmosphere, and although there are paths and tracks, some of them require greater concentration to follow; additionally, there are fewer signposts. The towns and villages of Sedbergh, Dent, Ravenstonedale and Tebay serve this area.

The north-east Dales, Swaledale and Wensleydale

This area contains fewer mountains but has excellent running terrain, with some of the best trail-running in the Dales. The two dales are rich in human history, especially in terms of lead mining. While the valleys are popular with tourists, the hills have relatively few visitors. This is especially true of the northern moorland section. Rights of way are marked on the map – although they are often small and indistinct on the ground. A good degree of self-reliance and navigational ability, therefore, is needed in poor weather. The area is served by the towns and villages of Hawes, Reeth and Leyburn.

The south-east Dales and Wharfedale

This very popular area features a mix of mountain and valley runs on mainly good paths and tracks. Wharfedale and its subsidiary valleys display the classic limestone scenery that the Dales is famous for, one of the highlights being Malham Cove and Gordale Scar, which regularly appear in television shows on the Dales. The area is served by the towns and villages of Grassington, Malham, Kettlewell and Skipton.

The Pendragon to Skipton Ultra

Most of the runs in this book can be readily achieved in a day. To provide a stiffer challenge the Pendragon to Skipton Ultra is a route designed to be spread over 1, 2 or 3 days depending on the runner. In this book, the ultra is described across three legs, which are described seperately as Route 19, Route 29 and Route 40. The route is not waymarked separately although sections of it follow Lady Anne's Way, the Pennine Way and the Dales Way.

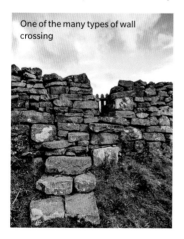

One of the many types of wall crossing

The route starts at Pendragon Castle in Mallerstang and finishes 85km later at Skipton station.

A linear route throws up challenges in terms of transport, the start and finish are linked by the Settle to Carlisle railway. The start is approximately 4km from Kirkby Stephen station and the finish close to Skipton Castle. The finish location for each leg are: Hawes, Kettlewell and Skipton respectively, all of which have a good selection of accommodation options and shops to re-supply.

Route descriptions

The run descriptions follow the same pattern: an introductory overview containing details of distance, ascent, start and finish points, points of interest, amenities and a brief overview of the route.

The descriptions generally state the nature of the route the run follows, namely, path, track or quad bike track, without noting whether it is classed as a footpath or bridleway. Most of the routes use a combination of footpaths, bridleways, and tracks or paths on open access land. For more information on access, visit www.yorkshire-dales.org.uk.

Most run descriptions refer to crossing several walls or fences; this means there is a crossing or gate of some type. Where appropriate, to aid navigation, the description is more specific, for example, 'cross using the ladder stile'.

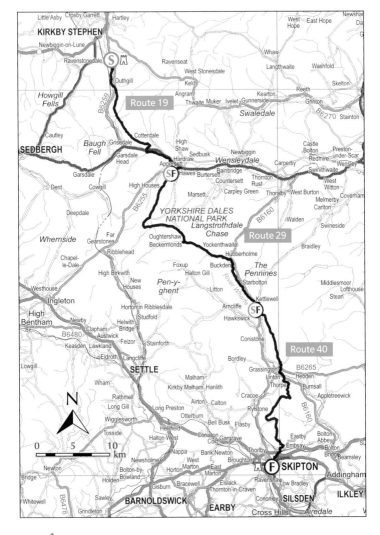

Mapping

The 1:50,000 OS map extracts indicate the route, and, together with the route description and gradient profile, should allow a competent runner to successfully complete the route. However, a full map of the area should also be carried.

Times and distances

A suggested time is given for each route, based on a speed of 8km per hour and 60 minutes per 1000m of ascent, rounded to the nearest half-hour. Individual speeds and fitness will of course vary. Runners will know their own speed over such terrain and be able to gauge how long each run should take. It is a good idea to run a couple of the routes and adjust your time accordingly. Factors that may affect the time taken include weather or navigational ability.

Each route is split into smaller sections; on shorter routes these roughly equate to 2km, and on longer routes, 4km. The sections are marked on the maps of each route. Where appropriate, grid references and distances are included. A cumulative distance is included at the end of each section, which was recorded using GPS. Inevitably, the distance will only be approximate, and towards the end of the route could differ by a few hundred metres, depending on exactly where you run. As such, they are intended as a guide only. Routes can be run in either direction; occasionally, the weather, for example, wind direction, dictates one way or the other. The run descriptions are probably the best way to run the route.

Run difficulty

Each run has been given a broad level of difficulty. The grade given to each run reflects the maximum level of difficulty on that particular route, even though some parts of the route may fall into a lower category of difficulty. Due to the nature of the terrain, some runs do not easily fall into a given category. Some runs comprise wide, easy-to-navigate paths with few signposts and vice versa. The more difficult runs include both navigational and route-finding aspects. Broadly speaking, navigational ability is about being able to read and follow a map. Route-finding ability is more about mountain experience and the ability to follow a route on the ground, being able to make a judgement about which direction to take. Where particularly relevant, a comment on safety has been included.

Level	Description
1	Well-signposted wide tracks and footpaths. No technical ground with medium ascents and descents. Straightforward navigation. May include short sections of road.
2	Well-signposted tracks and footpaths. Short sections of technical ground with steep(er) ascents and descents. Straightforward navigation.
3	Signposted smaller tracks and paths. Sections of technical ground with steep ascents and descents. Navigational ability necessary.
4	Small paths with few signposts. Mainly technical ground with steep ascents and descents. Navigational ability essential.
5	Small or intermittent paths with few, if any, signposts. Mainly technical ground with steep ascents and descents. Navigational and route-finding ability essential.

GPX tracks

GPX tracks for the routes in this guidebook are available to download free at www.cicerone.co.uk/922/GPX. A GPS device is an excellent aid to navigation, but you should also carry a map and compass and know how to use them. GPX files are provided in good faith, but neither the author nor the publisher accept responsibility for their accuracy.

THE SOUTH-WEST DALES AND THREE PEAKS

Leaders on the Settle Hills Race, 2017

Route 1
Settle Loop

Start/finish	Roadside lay-by, just off the Malham Tarn to Settle road: SD 830 652
Distance	13km (8 miles)
Ascent	440m (1440ft)
Grade	Level 2
Time	2hr
Terrain	A mixture of grassy paths and stone tracks with a few hundred metres of road
Map	OS Landranger 98: Wensleydale & Upper Wharfedale. OS Explorer OL2: Yorkshire Dales – Southern and Western Areas
Refreshments	A wide variety of shops, including two running/outdoor stores; cafés; and pubs in Settle
Public transport	Bus 580 from Skipton, 581 from Kirkby Lonsdale, 881 from Lancaster. Trains via the Settle–Carlisle railway line

A fast run, with little ascent and descent, around Langcliffe Scar. The run takes in the paths and bridleways between Settle and Malham, following the Settle Loop of the Pennine Bridleway for much of the route. From the start, the route climbs gently and traverses under the limestone outcrop of Attermire Scar. Many small outcrops and caves lie just off the route, and it is worth taking a torch to explore some of them if you have time.

The second section of the route passes above Stockdale Farm before climbing a track east towards Malhamdale, providing good views over Malham Tarn. The final section follows the Pennine Bridleway as it undulates back towards Settle to complete a circuit of Langcliffe Scar.

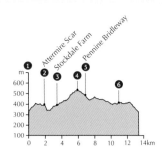

1 Take the track uphill, crossing over the cattle grid. Run ahead to reach a gate after three-quarters of a kilometre. Turn sharp R through the gate and pass through a smaller gate. Follow the path up and along the bottom of Langcliffe and **Attermire Scar**, passing **Victoria Cave**, to reach a second gate. Continue ahead and then descend a rocky path to the footpath junction 2km.

> ### The elephant in the cave
>
> When excavated, Victoria Cave was found to contain the bones of hippopotamuses, elephants and spotted hyenas from 130,000 years ago.

2 Turn L along the grassy path, passing through a small fenced area. Follow the grassy path alongside the wall to reach a small farm road. Turn L along the road for a few hundred metres. As the road descends to **Stockdale Farm**, look for the track on the L 3.6km.

3 Turn L through the gate and follow the rocky track up as it climbs the rough limestone plateau between Settle and Malham. As the path levels out, pass through a gate and run ahead to second gate. Continue ahead to a footpath junction 6km.

The rocky outcrops of Attermire Scar

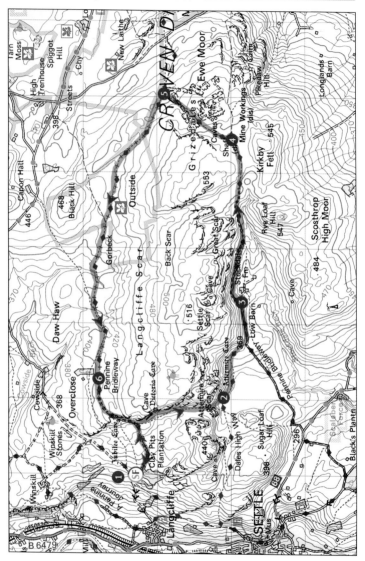

Last section of the Settle Loop with Pen-y-ghent and Fountains Fell behind

④ Turn L, following the footpath alongside the wall signposted 'Pennine Bridleway Langscar Gate'. Gradually descend in a NW direction across several fields and gates to reach a junction where the Pennine Bridleway joins a track 7.1km.

⑤ Turn L along the **Pennine Bridleway**, climbing gradually to a gate. Continue ahead following a good track as it undulates around the north side of the limestone plateau. Pass through several gates before running past a small patch of coniferous woodland 11.5km.

⑥ Continue ahead, as the track becomes more substantial, aiming for a small notch in the limestone escarpment. Pass through this and descend to meet the outward leg of the route at a gate. Continue to descend back to the starting point 13km.

Route 2
Crummackdale

Start/finish	Roadside parking near Austwick: SD 769 691
Distance	12km (7½ miles)
Ascent	325m (1070ft)
Grade	Level 3
Time	2hr
Terrain	A mix of grassy paths, walled lanes and fields
Map	OS Landranger 98: Wensleydale & Upper Wharfedale
Refreshments	Pub and shop in the village of Austwick
Public transport	Buses 580 and 581 from Skipton to Kirkby Lonsdale

This is a hidden gem of a route, featuring one of the best examples of Yorkshire Dales scenery. Crummackdale is often missed in favour of runs up the higher peaks of Ingleborough and Pen-y-ghent. The run is filled with geological interest, passing through the world famous Norber Erratics, as well as limestone pavement and layers of Moughton Whetstone, a banded mudstone used to make whetstones for razors. The run passes places such as Beggar's Stile and Thieves' Moss.

The run begins just outside the village of Austwick and climbs up on to the plateau east of Ingleborough, before following a short section of the Yorkshire Three Peaks route. The second half heads south and west, crossing through the limestone pavement of Moughton, before dropping back down to the start using an ancient walled lane.

1 Take the track W towards Clapham for 30 metres. Turn R over stile and run along the grassy track through the field to a wall. Turn R up to a wall corner. Cross through the small wooden gate and follow the path alongside the wall to the corner. Bear R and climb to meet a path. Turn R and follow the path for approximately 50 metres to a small, flat, grassy area and fingerpost. Turn

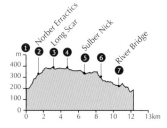

The moon setting over Norber

L, taking a small path up through a short rocky section. Bear R then L, following one of the small grassy paths diagonally N up through the **Norber Erratics** to a wall corner marked by a ladder stile at SD 765 702 1.2km.

Erratic deposits

The Norber Erratics are boulders of Silurian sandstone deposited by the last ice age. They lie on the surface, overlying the beds of limestone below.

---

2   Cross the wall and go straight ahead for a few metres to reach a small, stony path. Turn R and follow this path as it contours around the valley. After 400 metres, fork L on a grassy path heading for a notch in the limestone outcrop. Run through the notch and take one of the small paths heading N for approximately 500 metres, to reach a large cairn at **Long Scar**, adjacent to a grassy bridleway 2.8km.

3   From the cairn, run back to the bridleway and follow it NE to a bridleway junction. Continue ahead, following the Pennine Bridleway markers, to reach a gate crossing the track 4.8km.

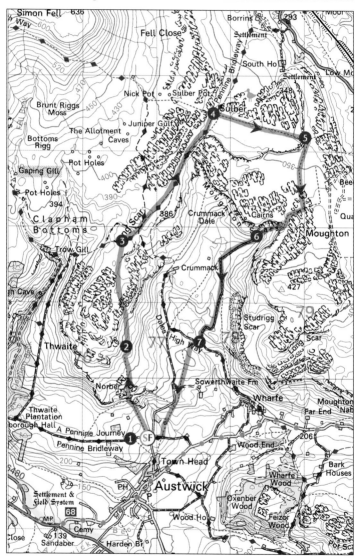

Running through the Norber Erratics (photo: Adrian Dellbridge)

4 Pass through the gate and continue ahead to reach the Sulber Nick path/ track junction. Turn R, signposted 'Horton in Ribblesdale'. Continue to follow this path for 1km before the path drops down to a gate. Continue ahead for 200 metres to a path junction and fingerpost 6.5km.

5 Turn R up the grassy path to a wall corner signposted 'Austwick'. Go through the gate and continue ahead, with the wall on your R, to a stile. Turn R, cross over the stile and follow the path to reach the head of **Crummackdale**. Descend the grassy path into the valley to reach the intake wall and gate 8.2km.

6 Run down the grassy track and walled lane for 2.5km to a track junction. Turn R and then L after 30 metres to cross the stream, using the lower of the two bridges 10.5km.

7 Follow the path up to the wall. Cross using the stone stile. Continue ahead as the path crosses several fields and stiles, and cross over a small stream using a small bridge. Follow the path up through the field to reach the track just below the starting point. Turn R back to the start 12km.

Route 3
Pen-y-ghent

Start/finish	National Park car park, Horton in Ribblesdale: SD 807 725
Distance	11km (7 miles)
Ascent	560m (1840ft)
Grade	Level 2
Time	2hr
Terrain	A mixture of good paths and tracks with a short section of road
Map	OS Landranger 98: Wensleydale & Upper Wharfedale
Refreshments	Pubs and café in Horton in Ribblesdale
Public transport	Train via the Settle–Carlisle line or Bus 11 from Settle

From some angles Pen-y-ghent has the profile of a sleeping lion or the sphinx rising high above upper Ribblesdale. The run is straightforward, reaching the summit of one of Yorkshire's iconic mountains in just a few kilometres. Pen-y-ghent is often the first peak climbed when walking/running the Yorkshire Three Peaks.

The route follows the main path ascending Pen-y-ghent from the west, summiting via the rocky southern escarpment. A short scramble completes the last few metres of the escarpment up on to the summit plateau. However, there is little to worry about and the section is soon over. The descent follows the paved/rocky summit path back towards Horton in Ribblesdale before taking advantage of the new Three Peaks path laid by the YDNP. This extends the run by a few kilometres and joins up with the Pennine Way to bring you back to the start.

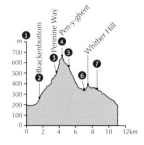

Safety

The last few metres of the steep climb on to the summit plateau involve an easy scramble. CARE should be taken in wet or wintry conditions.

Pen-y-ghent's profile

The steep rocky profile of Pen-y-ghent is caused by its geology. Layers of harder millstone grit cap bands of limestone and shales.

① Turn R out of the car park and follow the road past the Pen-y-ghent Café and then the campsite. Cross the road just before the **church** and turn L on the public footpath. Turn L along the road and then immediately R over the footbridge signposted 'Pen-y-ghent via Brackenbottom'. Turn L and run up the road, past the old primary school, out of the village to a farm 1.3km.

② Turn L before the farm, signposted 'Pen-y-ghent Summit'. Follow the well-worn footpath alongside the wall as it climbs steeply up through the fields. The gradient lessens and the route becomes a series of flat terraces interspersed with small limestone steps. Continue ahead for a couple of kilometres, heading for the foot of Pen-y-ghent summit (south side). The final

The steep final ascent up Pen-y-ghent (photo: Alice Ellwood)

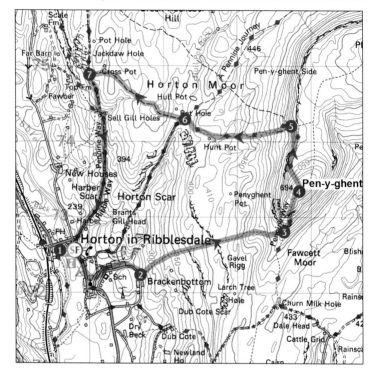

part of this section rises steeply up flagged stone steps to meet the **Pennine Way** 3.6km.

3 Turn L and climb the steep path that leads to the summit of **Pen-y-ghent**. The path climbs steeply then crosses a short, flat section before climbing very steeply to the summit plateau. Run across the plateau on a good paved path as it rises gently to Pen-y-ghent's trig point 4.3km.

4 Cross L through the wall and head NW downhill, taking a rocky path that soon becomes paved. The path bears R at the escarpment. Run down the rocky path along the edge and then down through the escarpment to a prominent bend in the path, marked with a Pennine Way signpost 5.3km.

Running on Pen-y-ghent's southern slopes
(photo: Alice Ellwood)

5 Continue to run downhill, following the Pennine Way down a gravel path. After a kilometre the angle lessens. Pass through a gate and continue down through a second gate to a major track junction signposted 'Pennine Way and Yorkshire Three Peaks 6.9km.

6 Run straight ahead, following a small gravel path signposted 'Yorkshire Three Peaks High Birkwith via Whitber'. This is a new path and may not appear on some maps. Follow the path as it ascends Whitber Hill. Turn L along the path as it crosses rough moorland and descends over a small stream. Follow the gravel path through a kissing gate and then downhill to reach a track junction signposted 'Yorkshire Three Peaks and Pennine Way' 8.6km.

7 Turn L through the gate, signposted 'Pennine Way, Horton in Ribblesdale'. Run along the grassy track to descend past a couple of ruined barns. Bear L through the gate over Sell Gill Pot stream. Run down the stony track, which becomes a walled lane as it drops back to **Horton in Ribblesdale**. The track emerges at the Crown Pub. Turn L back to the starting point 11km.

Route 4
The Three Peaks (Pen-y-ghent, Whernside and Ingleborough)

Start/finish	National Park car park, Horton in Ribblesdale: SD 807 725
Distance	40km (24¾ miles)
Ascent	1610m (5280ft)
Grade	Level 3
Time	6hr
Terrain	The route has a bit of everything but is mainly run on good paths, paved in places, and tracks with short grassy sections, as well as road sections. In recent years many of the paths have been upgraded, improving the conditions underfoot. However, the descent off Ingleborough can be boggy, muddy and rocky in places
Map	OS Landranger 98: Wensleydale & Upper Wharfedale
Refreshments	Pubs and café in Horton in Ribblesdale. Station Inn and seasonal tea van at Ribblehead. The Old Hill Inn at Chapel-le-Dale
Public transport	Train via the Settle–Carlisle line or Bus 11 from Settle

One of the classic long runs in the Yorkshire Dales, this route follows the Yorkshire Three Peaks route, which differs slightly from the route of the Three Peaks Fell Race. This route takes a better route to the summit of Pen-y-ghent, thereby avoiding the up-and-down repeat of the fell race. It also avoids the direct ascent of Whernside in order to reduce erosion on the race route. Reaching the summits of three of the highest mountains in the National Park involves a steep climb and is rewarded with panoramic views of the Dales and beyond, including the Lake District to the north and Pendle Hill to the south. Not to be underestimated, the route is just short of a marathon and includes three big ascents.

The route starts with the smallest of the three mountains, Pen-y-ghent, before taking in a long flatter section to Ribblehead. From here the route follows the Settle–Carlisle railway line for a short distance before climbing Whernside, the highest mountain in the Dales. A steep descent leads to Chapel-le-Dale and the Old Hill Inn, followed by a steep ascent of Ingleborough. The final section is the long gradual descent back to the start at Horton in Ribblesdale.

Safety

The last few metres of the steep climb on to Pen-y-ghent's summit plateau involve an easy scramble. CARE should be taken in wet or wintry conditions. In poor visibility navigating across Ingleborough's summit plateau can be difficult. Make sure you can safely navigate on to the correct path. In winter the escarpment and slabs can be covered by thick snow/ice. Spikes or crampons would be essential.

Start of the Three Peaks Race, Horton in Ribblesdale

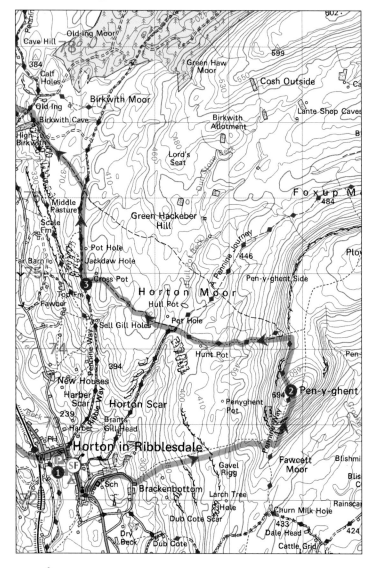

Stamp your card here

Horton in Ribblesdale is a starting point for the Yorkshire Three Peaks. The Pen-y-ghent Café houses an old clock card machine from a Lancashire mill, where you can stamp your card at the start and finish of your circuit. Completion within 12 hours enables you to become a member of the Three Peaks of Yorkshire Club.

1 Turn R out of the car park and follow the road past the Pen-y-ghent Café and then the campsite. Cross the road just before the **church** and turn L on the public footpath. Turn L along the road and then immediately R over the footbridge signposted 'Pen-y-ghent via Brackenbottom'. Turn L and run up the road, past the old primary school, out of the village to a farm. Turn L before the farm, signposted 'Pen-y-ghent Summit'. Follow the well-worn footpath alongside the wall as it climbs steeply up through the fields. The gradient lessens and the route becomes a series of flat terraces interspersed with small limestone steps. Continue ahead for a couple of kilometres, heading for the foot of Pen-y-ghent's summit (south side). The final part of this section rises steeply up flagged stone steps to meet the Pennine Way.

Turn L and climb the steep path that leads to the summit of **Pen-y-ghent**. The path climbs steeply then crosses a short, flat section before climbing very steeply to the summit plateau. Run across the plateau on a good paved path as it rises gently to Pen-y-ghent's trig point 4.3km.

The profile of Pen-y-ghent

2 Cross L through the wall and head NW downhill, taking a rocky path that soon becomes paved. The path bears R at the escarpment. Run down the rocky path along the edge and then down through the escarpment to a prominent bend in the path, marked with a Pennine Way signpost.

Continue to run downhill, following the Pennine Way down the gravel path. After a kilometre the angle lessens. Pass through a gate and continue down through a second gate to a major track junction signposted 'Pennine Way and Yorkshire Three Peaks'.

Run straight ahead, following a small gravel path signposted 'Yorkshire Three Peaks High Birkwith via Whitber'. This is a new path and may not appear on some maps. Follow the path as it ascends Whitber Hill. Turn L along the path as it crosses rough moorland and descends over a small stream. Follow the gravel path through a kissing gate and then downhill to reach a track junction signposted 'Yorkshire Three Peaks and the Pennine Way' 8.6km.

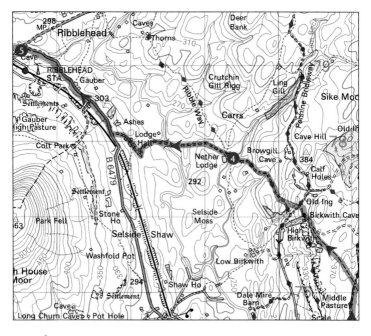

3 Turn R, signposted 'Yorkshire Three Peaks and High Birkwith'. Run along the grassy track as it climbs gently up Ribblesdale. After approximately a kilometre and a half turn L through a kissing gate. Follow the gravel path up and over to a wall crossing. Continue ahead through the fields, aiming for the R corner of a small conifer wood to meet a track. Bear L and descend to a gate. Bear R a short distance to meet a larger track. Descend past a Three Peaks marker post and cross a small stream. Follow the path over the grassy hill to a gate. Continue to run along the path through the fields to another gate and stream. Turn L through the gate and follow the track to the footbridge at **Nether Lodge** 12.4km.

4 Cross the bridge and follow the path around to the front of the farm. Turn R along the track, away from the farm, and follow this down to the bridge over the infant River Ribble. Run along the track and up through the farm to reach the **B6479**. Turn R and run along the road to the T junction at Ribblehead 16.4km.

5 Run along the track towards the viaduct. Just before **Ribblehead viaduct** Turn R, signposted 'Whernside', and run up the path and steps to a gate. Follow the track alongside the railway to the Blea Moor signal box. Run past the signal box, following the undulating track to a small stream. Continue to run along the track, crossing a second stream and wooden bridge. Shortly afterwards turn L over the railway and run up the track to a gate. Pass through the gate and climb steeply upwards, following a paved path as it climbs the lower slopes of Whernside. Follow the path for approximately 1km to a footpath junction 20.3km.

6 Turn L and follow the gravel path, paved in parts, over a series of terraces towards the summit ridge of Whernside. A steep final climb brings you to the ridge. Turn L and run up and along the ridge to Whernside's summit trig point at **736m** 23.4km.

7 From the summit descend the rocky path, heading S, to a gate. Run along the main path for approximately 1.5km. Turn L down the steep escarpment. Descend the steep path into the valley. CARE is needed at the top section. Run down the path to a gate and barn, between **Bruntscar** and **Broadrake**. Turn R and then immediately L through the farm. Run down the road through the fields past a conifer wood to cross a small stream (often dried

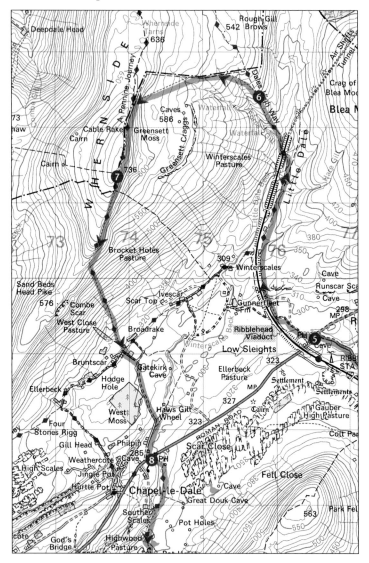

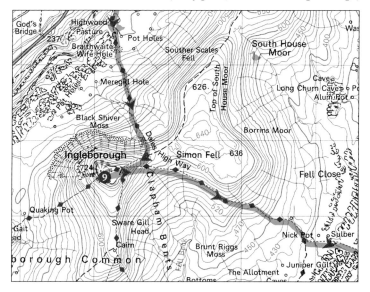

up). Bear R and follow the road until it meets the **B6255** (from Ingleton). Turn L towards the Old Hill Inn 27.9km.

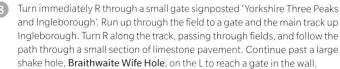

8 Turn immediately R through a small gate signposted 'Yorkshire Three Peaks and Ingleborough'. Run up through the field to a gate and the main track up Ingleborough. Turn R along the track, passing through fields, and follow the path through a small section of limestone pavement. Continue past a large shake hole, **Braithwaite Wife Hole**, on the L to reach a gate in the wall.

Run up the flagstone slab path (reclaimed from the mills of northern England; some of the machine fitting slots can still be seen) and across a short section of boardwalk. Continue to ascend over a small stream to climb again to the foot of a steep escarpment. Climb up the steep path and across the stream. Pass through the gate and turn R, following the steepening flagstone path. Just before the summit plateau you will pass the return route path junction on the L. Continue on to the plateau of **Ingleborough**. Cross the plateau, heading SW, to reach the trig point at **723m** and the cross-shaped stone shelter (SD 741 745) 32km.

9 Retrace the route across the top of the escarpment, heading NE to three large cairns on the northern edge of the plateau. Take care in poor visibility. It's very easy to become disorientated on the summit plateau. Use a map and compass. Run down the flagstone path back to the junction. Bear R and run down the flagged path towards Horton in Ribblesdale. At the end of the flagged section descend a steep and rocky section to a rough stone track. Follow this as it contours to the south of **Simon's Fell** to reach a wall crossing. Continue to run downhill on a rough path, interspersed with short flagged and boardwalk sections, to a small ruined building. Run past the ruin, crossing a small stream, to a gate. Pass through the gate and run a short distance to a junction. Bear L at the marker post and follow the muddy path alongside the wall and around a low rocky outcrop to the gate. Continue to run along the muddy and rocky path to reach the bridleway junction at Sulber Nick 36.4km.

10 Run down the gradually improving path, past occasional stone cairns, before dropping down a rocky section to a gate. Continue ahead, past a cairn and fingerpost, through a large gap in the wall. Bear R and follow the path, with the occasional marker post, through a rocky limestone section as it descends through the fields to a farm track. Cross the track and run up through the fields before dropping down to **Horton in Ribblesdale Station**. Cross the railway and run down the road. Bear R before the road bridge into the car park 40km.

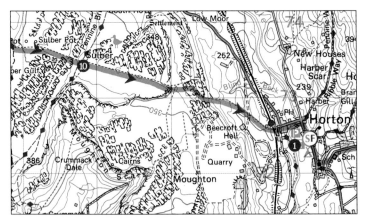

Route 5
Gragareth

Start/finish	Park at the roadside lay-by: SD 691 756
Distance	11.5km (7 miles)
Ascent	390m (1280ft)
Grade	Level 4
Time	2hr
Terrain	Grassy tracks, steep moorland and grass paths
Map	OS Landranger 98: Wensleydale & Upper Wharfedale
Refreshments	The Marton Arms and cafés, pubs and shops in Ingleton
Public transport	Buses 581, 833 and 881 to Ingleton are the closest

A straightforward run along an old green lane, followed by a steep ascent of one of Lancashire's highest hills. The route uses the old Turbary Road to contour above beautiful Kingsdale, before a short but steep ascent leads you to the summit ridge that links Gragareth and Great Coum. Gragareth's trig point is soon reached. From the summit there are panoramic views of Morecambe Bay, the Lake District and the Yorkshire Dales.

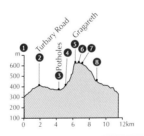

An ancient right

The term 'turbary' refers to the ancient right to cut peat for fuel. A Turbary Road was the road used to transport the cut peat. Beneath Kingsdale lies a labyrinth of caves and submerged passages, including the longest cave dive in the UK, which connects King Pot to the resurgence of Keld Head.

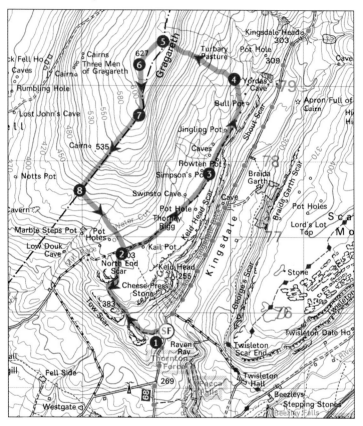

1. From the start, pass through the metal gate and run up the grassy track that zigzags to a gate. Run through the gate and follow the grassy track through a limestone escarpment to meet a track, the Turbary Road 1.7km.

2. Turn R and follow the flat grassy track to the gate. Go through the gate and run along the track, through several fields, to reach two potholes very close to the track. CARE is needed as the closest one is right next to the track 4km.

③ Run ahead, following the track along the wall side to another gate. Go through the gate and run uphill. Follow the track as it bears L down a small dip and then steeply up to a gate at SD 701 790 4.8km.

④ Turn L through the gate and follow the wall up a very faint path, which is boggy in places. After a couple of hundred metres pass an old stone sheep fold. The path now becomes very steep and rocky in places. Climb up to the summit ridge, passing a small rock outcrop, and continue for another 100 metres to reach the wall that runs lengthways along the summit ridge 6km.

⑤ Cross through the small wooden gate, bearing diagonally L and SW for 400 metres along a faint grassy path to the trig point at the summit of **Gragareth** 627m 6.5km.

⑥ From the trig point, bear L on a small grassy path S across the plateau back to the summit ridge wall. Bear R along the wall to a wall junction. Cross the wall using an old wooden ladder stile. Turn R and run a short distance to the next wall crossing 7km.

A frosty, grassy finish back down to Kingsdale
(photo: Adrian Dellbridge)

The broad slopes of Gragareth

7 Run downhill on a grassy path alongside the wall. After a few hundred metres the path descends more steeply to a broken wall. Continue to run downhill, across a small boulder field, to a second broken wall 8.5km.

8 Turn L and follow a faint, intermittent path along the broken wall. After a couple of hundred metres cross a small stream and run along past a small stand of trees, back to waypoint 2. From there retrace the outward route back to the start 11.5km.

Route 6
Ingleborough (from the Old Hill Inn)

Start/finish	Park on the roadside near the Old Hill Inn: SD 745 777
Distance	8.5km (5¼ miles)
Ascent	445m (1460ft)
Grade	Level 4
Time	1hr 30min
Terrain	A run through fields to start, followed by good paths to and from the summit. The final section includes a small, steep and occasionally slippy, grassy path that requires care. The run finishes back through the fields
Map	OS Landranger 98: Wensleydale & Upper Wharfedale
Refreshments	The Old Hill Inn, pubs, cafés and shops in Ingleton
Public transport	Bus 830 from Ingleton/Hawes

A classic route on paths and tracks with stunning views of Ingleborough, Whernside, and other hills of the Yorkshire Dales.

The run follows a section of the popular three peaks footpath from the Old Hill Inn through fields to Ingleborough's steep northern escarpment. The route then climbs the main ridge to the summit plateau and trig point. The return leg retraces the route to the top of the escarpment and then takes an alternative route north along the escarpment edge before dropping back down the fellside, passing Great Douk Cave, and back to the start.

Safety

In poor visibility navigating across Ingleborough's summit plateau can be difficult. Make sure you can safely navigate on to the correct path. In winter, the escarpment and slabs can be covered by thick snow or ice. Micro-spikes or crampons would be essential.

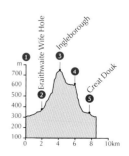

Runner finishing the Ingleborough route (photo: Alice Ellwood)

1. Passing through the gate from the road, run along the footpath through three fields and follow the path through a small section of limestone pavement. Continue past a large shake hole, **Braithwaite Wife Hole**, on the L to reach a gate in the wall 2km.

2. Go through the gate and run up the flagstone slab path (These were reclaimed from the mills of northern England; some of the machine fitting slots can still be seen.) and across a short section of boardwalk. Continue to ascend over a small stream to climb again to the foot of a steep escarpment. Climb up the steep path and cross a flagged bridge over the tiny stream. Pass through the gate and turn R, following the steepening flagstone path on to Ingleborough's plateau. Bear SW across the plateau to reach the trig point at **723m** and the cross-shaped stone shelter at SD 741 745 4.1km.

Distinctively flat

The distinctive flat summit of Ingleborough is due to its geology. The summit comprises millstone grit on top of a layer of limestone.

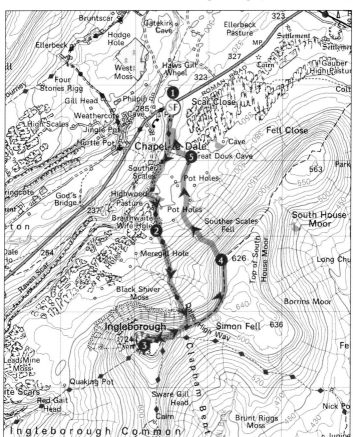

3 Retrace the route across the top of the escarpment, heading NE to three large cairns on the northern edge of the plateau. Take care in poor visibility. It's very easy to become disorientated on the summit plateau; use a map and compass. Run down the flagstone path back to and through the gate and across the stream. Do not descend L down the steep path. Instead, turn R and continue straight on, running along a small path that follows the edge of the escarpment. Follow this for over a kilometre to a wall crossing 5.9km.

Ingleborough's northern escarpment in winter

4 Turn L a few metres before the wall and descend steeply down a small rocky path. Continue to descend this very steep path, running parallel to the wall. The path improves as you get further down before reaching a small stone stile at a wall junction. Turn R over the stile, signposted by a red arrow, and run along a grassy path, with an occasional stone paving slab, to **Great Douk Cave**. There are several paths but all seem to lead to the same place. Great Douk is surrounded by a large circular stone wall 7.6km.

5 Turn L and run down a grassy track alongside the wall, following it to the main track. Turn R through the gate, signposted 'Sleights Road', rejoining the original route through the fields and back to the start 8.5km.

Route 7
Ingleborough (via Park Fell)

Start/finish	Plenty roadside parking at Ribblehead: SD 765 792
Distance	14km (8¾ miles)
Ascent	545m (1790ft)
Grade	Level 3
Time	2hr
Terrain	A mixture of grassy and rocky paths. A rocky section across the summit plateau is followed by a very steep stone-pitched path down the escarpment and flagstone path to the nature reserve trail. The route continues along a grassy path through rough pasture, boggy in places, back to the start
Map	OS Landranger 98: Wensleydale & Upper Wharfedale
Refreshments	Station Inn and ice cream/refreshments van (seasonal) at Ribblehead
Public transport	Bus 830 from Ingleton/Hawes or train via Settle–Carlisle railway line to Ribblehead

This route comprises a tour of Ingleborough starting from Ribblehead. The run climbs the steep northern slope of Park Fell. A 3km traverse of Ingleborough's impressive north-east ridge brings you to the summit plateau, followed by a short distance across the plateau to arrive at Ingleborough's summit trig point. The next section retraces the route for a short distance, before dropping down the steep escarpment on an excellent flagstone path. The final section follows a small waymarked path through limestone pavement and potholes to meet the outward route, a short distance from the start.

Safety

In poor visibility navigating across Ingleborough's summit plateau can be difficult. Make sure you can safely navigate on to the correct path. In winter the escarpment and slabs can be covered by thick snow or ice. Spikes or crampons would be essential. The descent path on the escarpment is steep and rocky. Take care when descending.

1 From the car park, run up the road past the Station Inn and under the railway bridge. Turn L along the track and enter the Ingleborough National Nature Reserve, by the information board opposite **Ribblehead Station**. On a clear day, you will able to see the wall running down from the summit of Park Fell to a junction. This is where you are aiming for. Follow the green markers of the Ribblehead Quarry Walk to a gate at SD 768 784. Pass through the gate and, after a few metres (just before the second green marker post), bear diagonally L along a small grassy path through the limestone pavement and grass-land to a second gate. Cross the stone step stile marked with a yellow-topped post and turn R, following the path round to a wall corner 2.1km.

Running along the escarpment path, Ingleborough's summit behind (photo: Andy Ward)

Did you know?

Ingleborough's National Nature Reserve and Site of Special Scientific Interest (SSSI) covers over a thousand hectares of the northern and eastern half of one of Yorkshire's famous three peaks.

---

2 Pass through the gate and, with the wall on your L, climb up the steep path to a wall junction. Cross over the stile and through the gate. Run along the path for a short distance to reach Park Fell's summit and trig point. Run back to the wall junction and stile. Turn L and follow the path, initially along the wall side, SW towards Ingleborough, to a fence and stile 3.5km.

3 Cross the fence and descend to the wall corner. Continue ahead, climbing steeply for a short section. Run along the small grassy path through the boulder field to a wall crossing above **Souther Scales Fell** 5.1km.

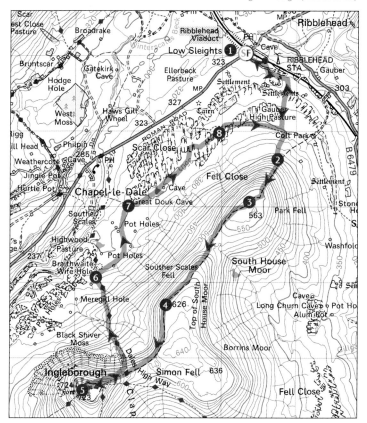

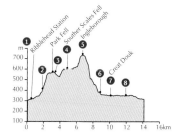

4 Continue ahead, following the escarpment edge, to a path junction and gate. (The path joining from the R is the main three peaks ascent path from the Old Hill Inn.) Pass through the gate and climb steeply up the path. Head towards the rocky outcrop that marks the summit plateau's

A section of the grassy path from Park Fell to Ingleborough

northerly point. Pass this outcrop by a small path on the R that leads to the plateau. Cross the plateau to the trig point on **Ingleborough** at 723m, SD 741 745, and the large cross-shaped stone shelter. Take care in poor visibility; many people have become disorientated on the summit plateau 6.8km.

5 Run back down the route to the gate and stream at the top of the escarpment. Cross the small stream and descend very steeply down a rocky path through the escarpment, heading for a flagstone path. Run down the stone path until it ends at the entrance to **Southerscales Nature Reserve** 8.9km.

6 Do not enter the reserve. Instead, turn R on a small grassy path and head towards a wall junction. Cross the wall, bearing L to a second wall. Bear R, heading for a clump of trees that mark **Great Douk Cave**. Bear R past the cave to a small wooden gate. Turn R to reach a second gate 10.2km.

7 Continue ahead along the wall side to a gate. Turn L through the gate, then R along the wall side, through small patches of limestone pavement, to a gate. Turn R to a second gate. Turn L and follow the track, bearing R at the fork to a small wooden gate 12km.

8 Bear diagonally L through the limestone pavement, heading for a second small gate. Continue ahead, following the path leading back to the outward route. This is rejoined at the stone step stile and yellow marker post. Turn L and follow the outward route back to the start 14km.

Route 8
Dodd Fell

Start/finish	Roadside parking near Gearstones: SD 782 802
Distance	19.5km (12 miles)
Ascent	470m (1540ft)
Grade	Level 4
Time	3hr
Terrain	A mixture of good stone tracks, with short sections of road. The ascent and descent of the Dodd Fell plateau is across rough moorland on small paths; this is frequently boggy
Map	OS Landranger 98: Wensleydale & Upper Wharfedale
Refreshments	Seasonal snack van and pub at Ribblehead
Public transport	Bus 830 to Far Gearstones from Ingleton/Hawes or train via Settle–Carlisle railway line to Ribblehead

A straightforward run up one of the Dale's central peaks. The route links sections of the Dales Way, Pennine Way and Pennine Bridleway, providing almost 20km of good running with excellent views of Langstrothdale and Upper Wharfedale. The first section of the route uses the Cam High Road, an ancient Roman road, to ascend from the valley to the bottom of Dodd Fell. A short section off-road takes you across a grassy plateau to the summit of Dodd Fell. The outward journey is retraced to the Pennine Way and Bridleway junction and descends, via the bridleway, to the Ingleton–Hawes road (B6255). A short road section leads you to a bridleway, which returns to the start.

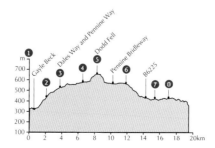

> ### Safety
> The summit of Dodd Fell is pretty featureless. If in doubt, continue past the turning point to a point due west of the trig point and ascend across the fell on a compass bearing. The turning point is at the second wall on the left, past the point where you should have left the track.

1 From the start, run up the road to the bend. Take care crossing the road and run down the track across **Gayle Beck**. Continue ahead, crossing a small stream. The run now climbs steeply, before levelling off, then climbing again to the Dales Way and Pennine Way track junction 2km.

2 Continue running uphill to reach a track fork. Take the L fork (straight on) through the gates. The track becomes stonier as it climbs up and around the hillside. Run ahead to a track footpath junction (where the Dales Way and Pennine Way separate) 3.7km.

3 Run ahead to reach another gate. Pass through the gate and climb up for a short distance, before descending to join the tarmac access road to Cam Farm. Run straight on to the cattle grid where the Pennine Bridleway joins on the L. Run along the road for a few hundred metres to a track junction and fingerpost 6.2km.

4 Turn L along the Pennine Way track. Follow the track alongside the wall for approximately 1km to a gate. Run straight on. Shortly after, look for a stone cairn on the hillside, approximately 30 metres up from the track and small stream gully. A small stone cairn next to the track marks the start of a faint grassy path. Leave the track and bear R, climbing steeply up to the cairn. Follow the path past the cairn to climb on to the summit plateau of **Dodd Fell**. Run along the grassy path – boggy in places – across the plateau to Dodd Fell's

Running up past the cairn that marks the path to Dodd Fell's summit (photo: Andy Ward)

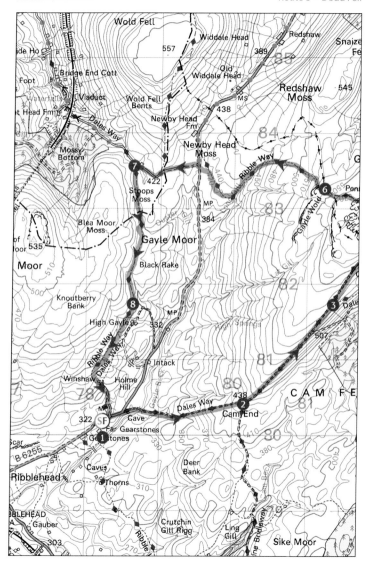

trig point at **668m**. Several paths lead to the summit. In good visibility, reaching the summit is straightforward. But in poor visibility it can be tricky 8km.

> ### Did you know?
>
> During the last ice age **Dodd Fell** was under the centre of a major ice sheet, estimated to be 1 mile thick.

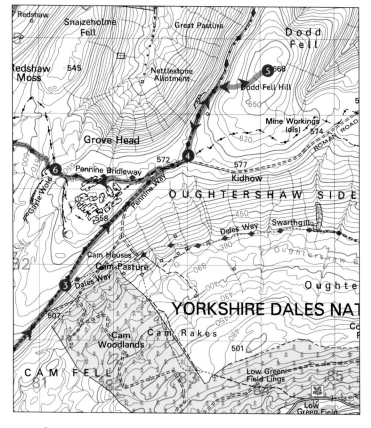

Other sports are available!

5   From the summit, run back across the plateau and descend to the track. Turn L and run back along the track to the road. Turn R and run along the road to the cattle grid crossed earlier. Do not cross the cattle grid, but turn R through the gate and immediately L to follow the grassy Pennine Bridleway over a small rise. After about 1km, the grassy track gives way to a stonier section. Continue downhill to pass through a gate 11.8km.

6   Pass through the gate and run down the stony track to the junction with the B6255. Turn R, then immediately L, signposted Dent. Run along the road for 1km, passing a rusty metal shelter on the R, to a bridleway junction on the L 15.3km.

7   Turn L along the small bridleway, signposted Gearstones. Run along the rocky, muddy in places, bridleway to a gate. Continue to run along the bridleway as it rises, before descending to a track/footpath junction by a farm 17.4km.

8   Bear R up the footpath, signposted Gearstones. Pass two small patches of conifers. Run along the path, around the edge of the farm, to a gate. Run along the boggy path alongside a wall, crossing over a couple of small streams and fences to a second farm. The path passes to the R of the farm to a track. Turn R takes you back to the start 19.5km.

Route 9
Cosh

Start/finish	Roadside parking near Gearstones: SD 782 802
Distance	27.5km (17 miles)
Ascent	745m (2450ft)
Grade	Level 5
Time	4hr
Terrain	A mix of broad stony tracks, grassy paths (boggy at times) and a short section of road
Map	OS Landranger 98: Wensleydale & Upper Wharfedale
Refreshments	Seasonal refreshments van at Ribblehead. Station Inn, Ribblehead
Public transport	Bus 830 to Far Gearstones from Ingleton/Hawes or train via Settle–Carlisle railway line to Ribblehead

A fantastic run, taking in the watershed of Wharfedale and Ribblesdale. The run combines sections of the Dales Way and Pennine Way, with a visit to the lonely trig point of Cosh. The first section uses the Cam High Road and the Dales Way to ascend from Ribblesdale up and over into Oughtershaw, through which flows one of the main tributaries of the River Wharfe. A short section of road leads to the other main tributary of the River Wharfe, Green Field Beck. A steep climb starts the next section: a traverse of High Green Field Knott and Cosh, running along small, sometimes intermittent, paths. This requires a high level of route-finding and hill craft in poor weather. The final section runs along the well-made paths and tracks of the Pennine Way, past Ling Gill and Cam End to return to the start.

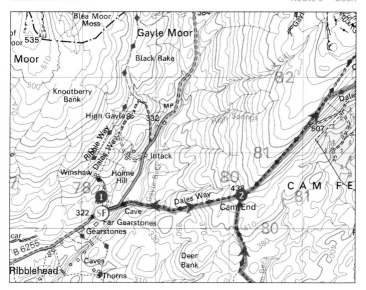

Historic high road

The Cam High Road was once used by Roman Legions travelling between Ingleton and the fort at Bainbridge.

1. Run up the road to the bend. Bear R down the track to Gayle Beck, cross the bridge and run along the track, crossing a small stream, before climbing steeply. After half a kilometre, the angle eases before kicking up again to **Cam End**, the track junction where the Dales Way and Pennine Way meet 2km.

2. Continue to run up the track over Cam Fell, following the Dales Way, to a gate. Pass through the gate, taking the L fork (straight on) through a second gate. Run along the track to a stone cairn that marks a footpath/track junction. Turn R down the small grassy and boggy path, across the rough pasture, heading for the farm at **Cam Houses**. Cross the forest access track and follow the small path to the farm 4.9km.

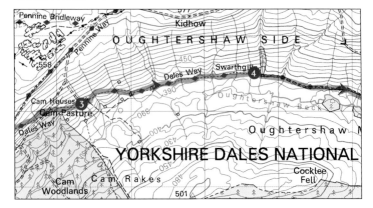

3 Follow the track around the L side of the farm, signposted 'Dales Way', through the farm buildings and down through the fields on a grassy path to a ruined, roofless barn. Turn L over a small stream and run along the Dales Way through several fields, over streams and small patches of regenerated woodland to reach the farm at **Swarthgill** 7.6km.

4 Take the track to the R of the farm, cross the stream and run down a rough tarmac track past Nethergill Farm to join a minor road at the hamlet of **Oughtershaw**. Turn R and run along the road, through Oughtershaw, before dropping steeply down to a road junction 11.8km.

The route through Cam Houses

⑤ Turn R and down the 'No Through Road' to Beckermonds. Turn L just after crossing over the road bridge and follow the track to a second river. Cross the foot bridge and turn R through a gate signposted 'Halton Gill'. Follow the grassy path steeply upwards past a stone barn and alongside a stream gully. The path is marked by an occasional way post. After a few hundred metres, the slope eases before climbing up again through moss-covered boulders. Bear L at a small cairn and follow the path to a second small cairn. Continue straight up, past a larger pile of stones to reach the summit ridge wall 14km.

⑥ Turn R (W) and run along the wall, following the intermittent path for a kilometre to a wall junction. Run ahead towards the grassy summit plateau, picking a route on either side of the broken wall, to reach a wall and fence

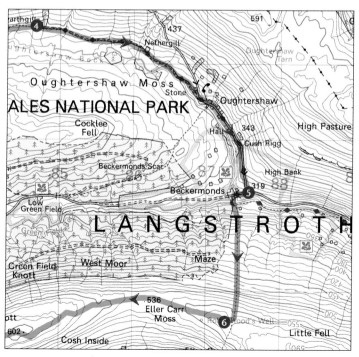

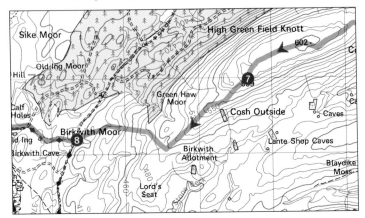

junction. Cross the fence and run alongside the wall, across the plateau, to a small gully. Cross this and bear L to the trig point of **Cosh** at 599m 18.2km.

7 From the trig point, bear L (SW) down the slope to a fence corner – electrified! Cross this and run over a small grassy shoulder, before bearing L again, down to pick up a small quad bike track. Run along the track to a junction of three walls, to the R of a small patch of conifer trees. Turn L at the wall junction and run along the quad bike track following the wall, which eventually runs out. Continue ahead past an old metal fuel tank and old wooden post. Follow the track as it turns R across rough moorland and over a small stream. Continue ahead over a small rise, dropping down to a gate. Pass through the gate and run straight ahead. After 50 metres, the track turns L. Instead, go straight on (W) down across the tussock moorland for approximately 500 metres to reach a wall. Turn L along the wall to a corner, with a small stream running through it. Here, cross to the far side of the wall. Turn L and follow the wall to meet the Pennine Way 22km.

8 Turn R along the Pennine way, following the path up and over to meet a forest access track. Turn L along the track to the track junction at **Old Ing**. Turn R and follow the Pennine Way to the limestone gorge of **Ling Gill** 24km.

9 Cross over the river bridge and run up the track as it rises away from the river. Continue to follow the track back to meet the outbound route at waypoint 2. Turn L and follow the track back to the start 27.5km.

Running past the cairn just past Cosh's summit (photo: Andy Ward)

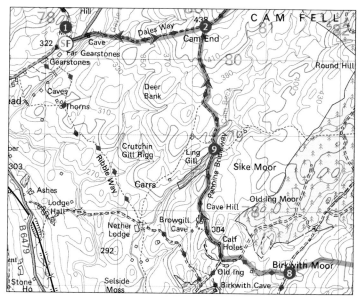

Route 10
Great Knoutberry

Start/finish	Limited roadside parking: SD 790 834
Distance	11.5km (7 miles)
Ascent	525m (1720ft)
Grade	Level 4
Time	2hr
Terrain	The route takes in a road section down into Dentdale, followed by a mixture of hard tracks and grassy paths climbing to the summit of Great Knoutberry. The Pennine Bridleway section back to the start is a mix of hard tracks and grassy paths
Map	OS Landranger 98: Wensleydale & Upper Wharfedale
Refreshments	Pubs, cafés and shops in Dent and Hawes; The Sportsman's Inn, Cowside
Public transport	Bus 830 from Ingleton/Hawes to Snaizeholme Lane End

Based around upper Dentdale, this route has a bit of everything, including a downhill start and finish. The first part of the run follows the road down into upper Dentdale, past the Settle–Carlisle railway line, to the hamlet of Stonehouse. Although you are on the road, it feels like you are running through the hills because of the good views of the northern Dales through to the Howgills and Baugh Fell. A stiff climb, which follows an ancient track under the magnificent Arten Gill Viaduct, leads up on to the open fell. Next comes an out-and-back section to the grassy summit of Great Knoutberry, before finishing with an undulating run along the Pennine Bridleway, back to the start. The summit of Great Knoutberry has good views north towards the Lake District and the Howgill Fells.

1 From the start, run down the road into Dentdale. Bear R after 100 metres and run past an old corrugated iron shed on the R. After just over a kilometre, pass an area of forest before dropping steeply down under the **Settle–Carlisle railway**. Continue to run down the road to the valley bottom, past the sign for Cowgill. Bear R along the road through the narrow, wooded valley to the white **Bridge End Cottage** 2.2km.

2 Continue to run down the road, passing the impressive white Dee Side House. The road runs alongside the infant River Dee to the small hamlet of Stonehouse. The route alongside the river is delightful, passing small waterfalls and old stone-arch bridges. As you near **Stonehouse**, the first view of Great Knoutberry appears, looming above Arten Gill. Continue to run down the road to Stonehouse 3.5km.

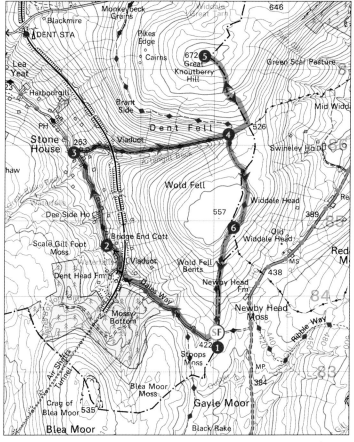

Winter conditions on the summit of Great Knoutberry

A berry by any other name...

Great Knoutberry comes from an alternative name for the cloudberry, a plant found in the sub-arctic tundra.

---

3 Turn R at Stonehouse, up the tarmac track, past the farm and old mill buildings, signposted 'Arten Gill', towards the viaduct. At the end of the tarmac section, pass through a gate and climb steeply up the stony track towards **Arten Gill viaduct**. The track steepens for a few hundred metres, before becoming less steep as you reach the viaduct. Continue to run up the track, now a walled lane. Climb for approximately 2km, out on to the open fell, to reach a bridleway crossroads. The signpost marks the point where the Pennine Bridleway (shown by an acorn symbol) crosses the track to Widdale 5.8km.

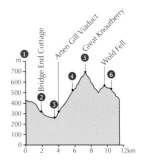

Looking up towards Arten Gill viaduct

4 Continue along the original track for a couple of hundred metres to reach a wall corner (spot height **526m**), where the track levels off at the col between Great Knoutberry and Wold Fell. Turn L over the stone stile and follow the grassy, sometimes boggy, path alongside the wall as it climbs up to the flat grassy summit of **Great Knoutberry**. The summit is marked by a small trig point at **672m** 7.3km.

5 Turn sharp R over the fence, using the wooden stile, and follow a faint grassy path, on the opposite side of the wall, downhill back to the track. Turn R and run along the track, back to waypoint 4. Turn L, signposted 'Pennine Bridleway' and run down this short section, before climbing over the grassy shoulder of **Wold Fell**. Run along a fantastic grassy section to reach a gate 10.2km.

6 Run along the grassy track to a second gate, pass through the gate and descend the stony track back down to the start 11.5km.

Route 11
Whernside (from Ribblehead)

Start/finish	Park in lay-by near Ribblehead: SD 765 792
Distance	13km (8 miles)
Ascent	715m (2350ft)
Grade	Level 3
Time	2hr
Terrain	Excellent stony tracks and paths with a short grassy section through fields
Map	OS Landranger 98: Wensleydale & Upper Wharfedale
Refreshments	Station Inn and seasonal tea van at Ribblehead
Public transport	Bus 830 from Ingleton/Hawes or train via Settle–Carlisle railway to Ribblehead

This route forms a classic run to the summit of Yorkshire's highest peak. Whernside is a large whaleback of a mountain standing high above the surrounding fells. It is climbed by thousands of people each year as part of the Yorkshire Three Peaks challenge. The route starts by passing the Ribblehead viaduct and then runs parallel to the railway before climbing up on to Whernside's northern ridge, following this to the summit trig point. The next section descends the southern section of the ridge before descending steeply to the valley. The final section runs along footpaths and tracks through fields and farms, back towards and under Ribblehead viaduct to the start.

 Run along the track towards the viaduct. Just before **Ribblehead viaduct**, turn R, signposted 'Whernside'. Run up the path and steps to a gate. Follow the track alongside the railway to the Blea Moor signal box. Run past the signal box, following the undulating track, to a small stream 2.1km.

Did you know?

The iconic 400m-long Ribblehead viaduct, and its 24 arches spanning Batty Moss, was built between 1870 and 1874, with up to 1000 navvies working on the site.

---

2 Continue to run along the track, crossing a second stream via a wooden bridge. Shortly afterwards, turn L over the railway and run up the track to a gate. Pass through the gate and climb steeply upwards, following a paved path as it climbs the lower slopes of Whernside. Follow the path for approximately 1km to a footpath junction 3.9km.

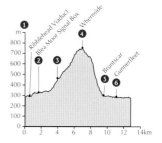

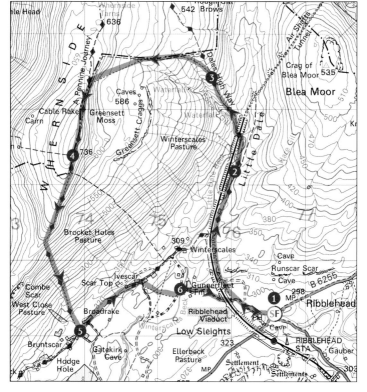

Looking across to Ingleborough above a cloud inversion

3. Turn L and follow the gravel path, paved in parts, over a series of terraces towards the summit ridge of **Whernside**. A steep final climb brings you to the ridge. Turn L and run up and along the ridge to Whernside's summit trig point at **736m** 6.8km.

4. From the summit, descend S on a rocky path to a gate. Run along the main path for approximately 1.5km. Turn L down the steep escarpment. Descend the steep path into the valley. CARE is needed at the top section. Run down the path to a gate and barn, between **Bruntscar** and **Broadrake** 9.5km.

5. Turn L past the barn and run along the grassy footpath through fields to a farm. Follow the path around the barn and through more fields to **Ivescar**. Turn R through the farmyard and then immediately L on a grassy footpath through the field to a wall. Cross the stone stile and through more fields to meet a farm access road. Turn L and follow the road to Gunnerfleet Farm 11.3km.

Running up the flagged path on the way to the summit

6. Turn R over the bridge and run along the track through the farm, heading back towards **Ribblehead viaduct**. Pass beneath the viaduct and take the track back to the start 13km.

THE NORTH-WEST DALES AND HOWGILLS

Running alongside one of the Whernside Tarns (Route 13)

Route 12
Dent to Ribblehead

Start	Dent Station: SD 763 875
Finish	Ribblehead Station: SD 766 790
Distance	14.5km (9 miles)
Ascent	500m (1640ft)
Descent	545m (1790ft)
Grade	Level 2
Time	2hr
Terrain	A short section of road leads from the station, followed by a mixture of grassy paths and stony tracks
Map	OS Landranger 98: Wensleydale & Upper Wharfedale
Refreshments	Station Inn, Ribblehead, and the Sportsman's Inn, Cowside, Dentdale
Public transport	Train to Dent Station

This linear route takes advantage of the train from Ribblehead Station to Dent (8 min). The first section starts at Dent Station, descending into the valley, before traversing west down the valley, via fields and farm tracks, following the Dales Way. The yellow Dales Way markers reduce the amount of potentially tricky navigation. The middle section runs south-east and ascends the Great Wold, up an ancient droving track. This section is fantastic, providing excellent running along a grassy track with good views of three dales. The final section runs alongside the Settle–Carlisle railway line, back to the start, passing the famous Ribblehead viaduct to finish at Ribblehead Station.

Linking old with new

The run links two established routes: one new, the Dales Way, created in 1968, which links Ilkley in Wharfedale to Bowness-on-Windermere; one ancient – the old droving track from Dentdale to Ribblesdale, which used to convey cattle to the fairs at Gearstones.

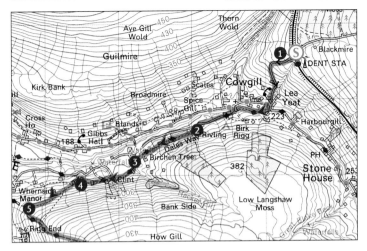

1　Turn L out of **Dent Station** and follow the road steeply down to the valley floor. Cross the infant River Dee, using the road bridge and immediately turn R through a gate to run alongside the river, signposted 'Ewegales Bridge'. Follow the river for a few hundred metres, reaching a road through a small **campsite**. Turn L and run along the road. After half a kilometre, bear L through the field, taking a footpath signposted 'Laithbank'. The path passes below and around the farm to the edge of a newly planted forest 2.2km.

2　Run through the wood, and below a second farm. Bear L across the field, heading for a stile in the top L corner. Continue back into a wood, following the yellow Dales Way route markers, and run past an old stone barn to a gate at the corner of the wall. Run down alongside a wall to meet a concrete track. Bear L for 50 metres, then turn R into the field. Run through the fields, before reaching a track 3.2km.

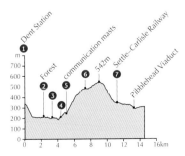

The grassy track between Dentdale and Ribblehead

3 Turn L and run a short distance to a track junction. Turn R, following a track over the stream and past a house on the L. Turn R, following a signposted path diagonally L to a kissing gate. Turn R and follow the wall, passing above the farm. Cross the stile and turn L to the next farm. Turn R along the farm track. After 100 metres continue ahead through a small gate, as the track turns R, to another farm. Run through the fields, past a farmhouse, to a large old barn. Bear L to a small wooded stream, followed by a large stone barn to a path and track junction 4.3km.

4 Here, the Dales Way turns R. Instead, run a short distance up the track to the farm. Turn L and take a small path up and around the farm. Continue through two small fields, bearing L to a wall and fence junction marked by trees. Traverse up to the L, signposted 'Craven Way', then R along the wall through a rough reed-filled field to a ladder stile. Cross the stile and bear L uphill to a second stile. Cross this stile and climb across another very rough field to a metal communications mast and a track. The tricky navigation is now over 5.3km.

5 Turn L and follow the steep track uphill, past the communication masts, climbing out of Dentdale. After 1km the track levels out and becomes a grassy walled lane. Follow the lane to the end at SD 745 846 7.5km.

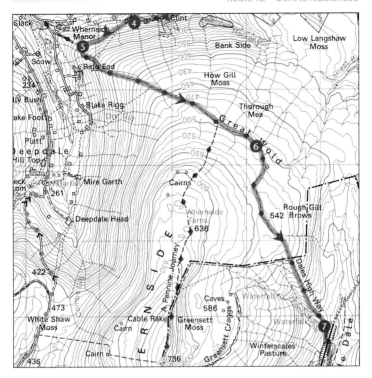

6 Continue to run along the grassy track, past an old derelict barn, to reach the high point of the route at **542m**. Run across the watershed to descend into **Little Dale**, meeting up with the popular tourist path up Whernside. Run down the path to the **Settle–Carlisle railway line** 11km.

7 Turn R across the railway and follow the stone track S, parallel to the railway line. Continue ahead for 1km, passing the Blea Moor signal box. Run along the track to the **Ribblehead viaduct**. Turn L in front of the viaduct and take the track to the road. Turn R, then L to **Ribblehead Station** car park 14.5km.

Fantastic wildflowers in Dentdale

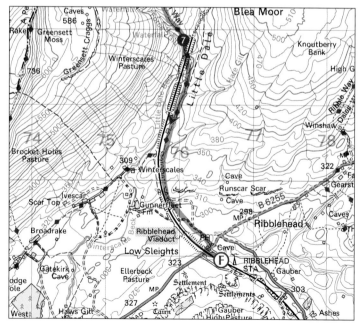

Route 13
Whernside (from Dent)

Start/finish	National Park car park, Dent: SD 703 871
Distance	19.5km (12 miles)
Ascent	655m (2150ft)
Grade	Level 3
Time	3hr
Terrain	A mixture of riverside paths, rocky tracks, small mountain paths and a short section of road
Map	OS Landranger 98: Wensleydale & Upper Wharfedale
Refreshments	Cafés, pubs and shop in Dent
Public transport	Bus S1–4 from Sedbergh/Kendal

This is a tough route that ascends Whernside via its northern ridge. The first section starts with a gentle run along the River Dee, before a stony track ascends the Great Wold. The middle section crosses wild open fell, climbing past isolated tarns high on Whernside's northern shoulder. The summit is reached by following the ridge path, before a superb grassy path descends into Kingsdale. The final section starts with a short section of road, which becomes a walled track, known locally as the Occupation Road, running beneath the eastern flank of Great Coum. A final stony descent of Flintergill brings you back to the start.

Did you know?

Dent was the birthplace of Adam Sedgwick, one of the founders of modern geology. For those who wish to make a visit, the Sedgewick Geological Trail is nearby in Garsdale.

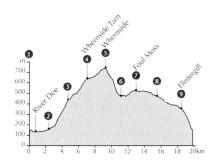

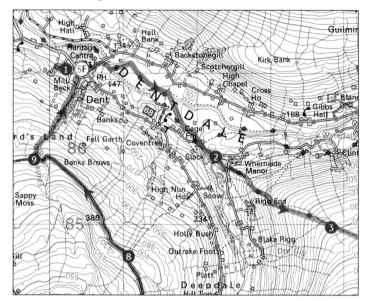

1 Turn L out of the car park and on to the cobbled street. Bear L on a footpath that passes in front of the **church** before rejoining the road. Turn L and run down towards the River Dee. Turn R before the river, signposted 'Mill Bridge', and follow a grassy path between the river and the fields. Turn L over a small bridge and bear R to a small gate marked with a Dales Way sign. Continue to run alongside the river to a fork. Bear R at the fork and continue to follow the smaller stream up through the fields to a kissing gate. Pass through the gate to meet a road 2.3km.

2 Turn L along the road, as it rises alongside a small conifer plantation, continue to a T junction and Turn R on to the 'No Through Road' and follow this for a couple of hundred metres. Turn L on to a track, signposted 'Ribblehead'. Run up the walled lane to a gate. Pass through the gate and follow the track steeply up, past the communication masts, to a gate. Continue up the steep, rocky track for approximately 1km, before the slope eases and the ground underfoot improves, to reach another gate 4.7km.

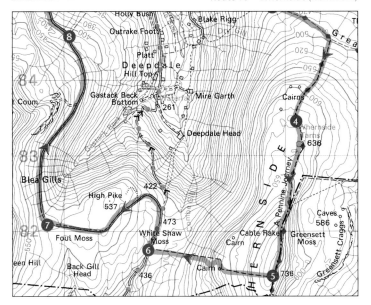

3 Run up the walled lane, through more gates, climbing on to the northern shoulder of **Whernside**. Continue to a gate and sheep folds. Pass through this and follow the track along the wall side for 100 metres to a wall corner (SD 746 845). Turn R and run uphill on a small path and quad bike track. Follow the path to the wall corner. Continue to follow the path past a small stone cairn to reach the most northern of the **Whernside Tarns** 6.8km.

4 Bear L around the tarn and run along a small grassy, boggy path that rises gently uphill. Run past a second smaller tarn and continue to bear L, to reach the wall and fence junction on Whernside's eastern escarpment (SD 740 823). Cross the fence using the stile on to the main 'tourist' path up Whernside. Turn R and follow the path steeply up hill to reach Whernside's summit ridge. Run along the ridge to the summit, cross through the wall to Whernside's trig point at **736m** 9km.

5 At the trig point turn R and, heading W, run downhill on a small rocky path for a couple of hundred metres to reach the top of a steep bank. Descend steeply and follow the path past three stone **cairns**. Turn R and follow the grassy path to a wall corner. Turn L and run down the grassy hillside, following a path and quad bike track parallel to the wall, crossing the boggy lower section to reach a small stream. Cross the stream to meet a road 11km.

6 Turn R and run along the road, uphill at first, to the junction of a road and track. Turn L, signposted 'Barbondale'. Follow the rocky track up and around the old quarry workings on High Pike. Continue to run along the track across **Foul Moss** to a small stream 13.2km.

7 Bear R on the boggy track to enter a walled lane, heading back in the direction of Dent. The next kilometre or so is rough going; the track is at times boggy and rocky. Follow the track as it runs along the eastern edge of **Great Coum**. After passing a series of fenced sheep folds, the going improves. Continue to descend to a second gate beneath a rocky outcrop. Pass through the gate and run down the track to a sharp L bend and footpath junction 15.2km.

8 Bear L along the track, signposted 'Kildershaw', and run along the track as it skirts under the northern slopes of Great Coum. Continue to follow the track. Eventually, it sweeps around a corner and over a small stream up to the **Flintergill** track junction 18.3km.

9 Turn R through the gate, down the track to a second gate. Run down the steep, stony track, through the wooded valley, back to the outskirts of **Dent**. Continue ahead through the houses, passing the village green on the R back to the start 19.5km.

Views across one of the Whernside Tarns

Route 14
Barbondale

Start/finish	Roadside parking next to a footbridge: SD 656 828
Distance	16.5km (10¼ miles)
Ascent	950m (3120ft)
Grade	Level 5
Time	3hr
Terrain	Mainly soft grassy running on small paths, with a couple of short sections on tracks. The run includes a very steep ascent and descent of fells on the eastern side of Barbondale
Map	OS Landranger 98: Wensleydale & Upper Wharfedale
Refreshments	The Barbon Inn; Barbon village shop; shops, pubs and cafés in Dent and Kirkby Lonsdale
Public transport	No nearby transport links

This is a tough route that is virtually all off-road. The route starts with a steady run up to Bull Pot Farm, followed by a runnable drag up to the top of Crag Hill. A short traverse to Great Coum is followed by a long descent to the Occupation Road: the name given to the track running north of Great Coum. This section needs good navigational and route-finding skills. There is a short section before a 300m (1000ft) ascent on to the Barbondale ridge. The route now turns south-west, with excellent running on soft ground, before plunging 1000ft back down to the start. This route is all on access land, and dogs are not allowed at certain times of the year. Check the notice board at the start for details.

Safety

Before you start, it is worth looking up at the final descent. Make sure you are happy ascending and descending this type of gradient. If not, a reasonable alternative is to run back down the valley on the road from waypoint 6.

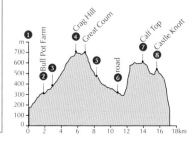

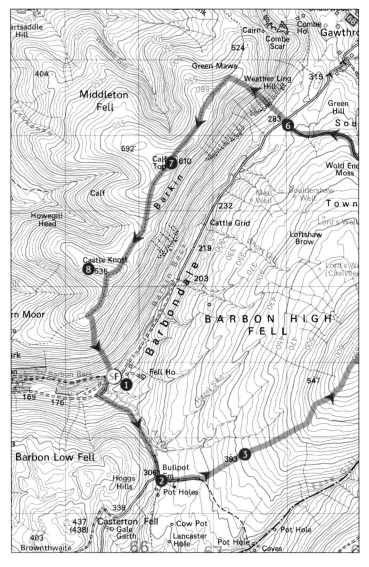

Running past the old trailer on the ascent of Crag Hill (photo: Andy Ward)

1. From the start, turn R and run back down the road towards Barbon for 300 metres. Turn L up the bridleway. Run up the stony path to a gate. Pass through the gate to reach the road. Turn L to **Bull Pot Farm** 1.9km.

2. Turn L past Bull Pot Farm, taking a walled track on to the fell. As the walled lane finishes (currently at an old horse trailer), bear L. Run up a grassy quad bike track, following the wall, to reach a gate after a few hundred metres 2.9km.

3. Pass through the gate and run up an indistinct grassy path to the summit fence. Bear R and follow the fence up the final summit section. Cross the wall to **Crag Hill** trig point at 682m 5.3km.

4. From the trig point, run along a small grassy path, occasionally crossing the wall, for 1km to the summit of **Great Coum** 687m, marked by a small stone cairn. From here take a line heading N down the fellside. Descend the escarpment, heading for a stream gully. Run down the L of the gully to pick up a quad bike track running parallel to a wall. Follow the wall to reach an old concrete foot bridge 8.2km.

5 Turn R through the gate and run down a walled track to meet the Occupation Road: a stony track that contours around Great Coum. Turn L along the track and follow it to the road 10.9km.

A road through history

The Occupation Road was built around the time of the Enclosure Acts, although the route dates back to an earlier time, when it facilitated access to coal mines and peat diggings. The stony track contours around Great Coum, from Kingsdale in the east to Barbondale in the west.

6 Turn R. After a few metres turn L through a gate. Ascend steeply straight up, following small sheep trods (paths) to the summit fence and wall. Turn L and run along the ridge to the trig point at **Calf Top** 610m 12.5km.

7 Descend the grassy path to a fence corner. Bear L and run down the grassy ridge. Cross a boggy section and ascend **Castle Knott** 15.4km.

8 Descend again to a small col above the start. Climb up to the stone cairn and descend, with care, the steep hillside straight down back to the start 16.5km.

Crag Hill trig point looking north to the Howgills (photo: Adrian Dellbridge)

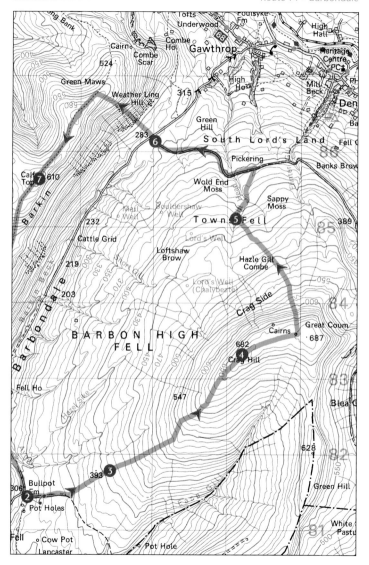

Route 15
Black Force (Howgills)

Start/finish	Roadside parking at Carlingill Bridge: SD 624 995
Distance	9.5km (6 miles)
Ascent	555m (1820ft)
Grade	Level 5
Time	1hr 30min
Terrain	A mixture of small grassy paths alongside Carlin Gill; short sections of rocky stream valleys, rough grassland and broad paths and quad bike tracks on the Howgills
Map	OS Landranger 97: Kendal and Morecambe
Refreshments	Pubs, shops and cafés in Sedbergh
Public transport	No nearby transport links

This route is a wild adventure of a run that follows narrow paths to reach the impressive waterfalls of Black Force and The Spout, before a rocky climb leads out into one of the high valleys of the Howgills. The second section crosses Docker Knott, Wind Scarth and Fell Head. This is typical Howgills terrain: excellent running along broad grassy ridges above steep-sided valleys. The final section is a long grassy descent down Linghaw to the start. Nesting bird restrictions may apply between late February and mid May. It is not advisable to undertake the run after periods of heavy rain, when crossing the stream may be impossible.

Safety

In poor weather, this run requires a high level of mountain craft and navigational ability, as it easy to become disorientated on the grassy, featureless ridges. The climb out from the bottom of The Spout needs care, as a slip could lead to a fall back into the rocky stream bed (see photo for route).

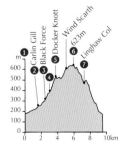

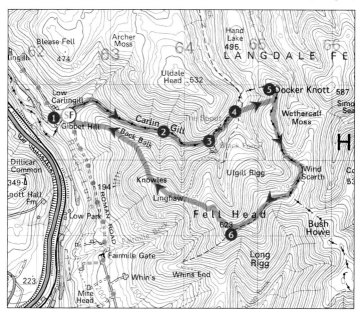

① Run down the road for a few metres. Turn R up a grassy track. Bear L at track fork, then L again on to a smaller grassy path heading into **Carlin Gill**. Run along the path before descending into Carlin Gill after a couple of hundred metres. Bear R and run along the narrow path on the R side of the stream. Take care crossing the occasional rocky step. Drop down to the stream and run up the small grassy path. After about 1.5km, cross a small stream and continue to a point opposite the place where two small streams enter Carlin Gill 1.6km.

② Continue ahead, following the small path up the narrowing valley. Cross another small stream and then cross to the L side of Carlin Gill. The path narrows as it climbs up and traverses above a small wooded rocky gorge Take CARE during this section. Continue alongside the river, passing small waterfalls and cascades for approximately 100 metres, to meet the stream that courses down the impressive rocky gully from **Black Force** 2.3km.

> **Did you know?**
> Black Force and The Spout are two of the finest waterfalls in the Howgills.

3 Run up the narrowing rocky gorge, crossing from the L to R bank along the intermittent path. After 100 metres, pass through a narrow boulder choke and continue ahead to reach a recess at the bottom of an impressive, high waterfall (The Spout). CAREFULLY climb up past the tree and ascend the steep grassy slope for a few metres on a very small path. Bear L and continue to follow the path, around the base of a rock slab, and climb up to meet a second path. Turn R and climb up and out of the rocky valley into the grassy valley above the waterfall. Cross from the R to L bank as necessary, following the stream up into the upper valley. Continue ahead to reach a stream junction 3.1km.

4 Climb up the grassy nose between the two streams and bear R for a short distance to a path. Follow the grassy path for approximately 100 metres, heading towards the stream gully coming down on the R. Turn R and climb up a small path on the R of the stream gully, to reach the col south of Docker Knott. Bear L at the col to join a larger path that leads up a steep bank to **Docker Knott** summit, marked by a few stones 3.8km.

Approaching the 'Spout'

5 Retrace the route back to the col and run along the grassy path, around the L side of Over Sale, to a second col. From here, climb up the grassy slope, on a good path, to the summit of **Wind Scarth**. Bear R as the slope eases and run up along the grassy ridge. Bear L around a

Flags marking the route out of the gorge

small grassy lump to meet a larger path. Turn R and run along the ridge for a few hundred metres to a stone cairn on **Fell Head** at 623m 6km.

6 Bear R downhill on a path for a short distance, before a short uphill section leads to a second smaller cairn. Bear R down the path to join a larger path down the broad spur. After a couple of hundred metres, bear L down to Linghaw col, which is crossed by a public footpath 7.2km.

7 Run up the steep bank to gain the summit of **Linghaw**. Continue ahead and run down the long, broad ridge, steep in places, back towards the start. Bear L at the bottom until the track peters out. Continue ahead to the road. Turn R along the road to the start 9.5km.

Route 16
Bowderdale

Start/finish	Limited roadside parking under the road bridge under the A685: NY 683 050
Distance	20km (12½ miles)
Ascent	1110m (3640ft)
Grade	Level 5
Time	3hr 30min
Terrain	Mainly grassy paths and tracks. There is a short section where the paths are intermittent or non-existent. The run starts and finishes with a short section of road
Map	OS Landranger 98: Wensleydale & Upper Wharfedale and OS Landranger 91: Appleby-in-Westmorland. The OS Explorer OL19: Howgill Fells & Upper Eden Valley 1:25000 would be useful in poor weather
Refreshments	Pubs in Ravenstonedale; café in Newbiggin-on-Lune
Public transport	Bus 571 (to Newbiggin-on-Lune) from Kendal

This route comprises a classic Howgills run around a remote valley, encompassing broad grassy ridges with steep ascents and descents. The first section runs south on grassy tracks and paths, along the western side of Bowderdale to The Calf: the highest point in the Howgills. The navigationally trickier middle section crosses the head of Bowderdale to climb steeply up Yarlside. The final section follows the eastern edge of Bowderdale, climbing up the steep smaller peaks of Kensgriff and Randygill Top. The run finishes down an excellent grassy track that leads you back to the start.

Safety

In poor visibility, the run is a serious one, requiring high levels of navigation and route-finding. Consider using a 1:25,000 scale map (OS Explorer OL19: Howgill Fells & Upper Eden Valley) in these conditions. The steep nature of the grassy ascents and descents makes studded fell shoes a must.

Ascending Yarlside (photo: Simon Oxley)

Did you know?

The Howgill Fells are formed from Silurian sandstone and mudstone, creating smooth steep-sided valleys, very different to the limestone and gritstone fells of most of the Yorkshire Dales.

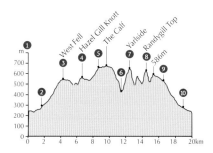

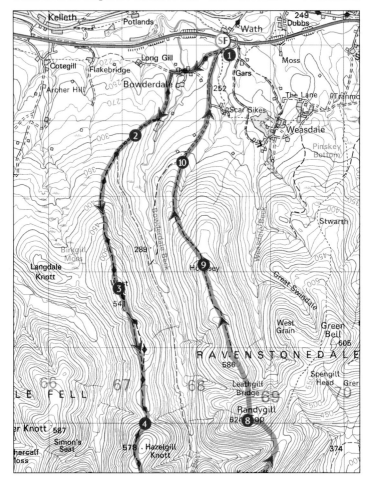

From the start, run down the 'No Through Road' over the cattle grid. Turn R at the junction signposted 'Bowderdale'. Run through the hamlet of **Bowderdale**, over the river and up the road. Turn L at the cattle grid and run along the bridleway. Continue to follow the track past two patches of conifers. Bear R and climb up to a gate 1.8km.

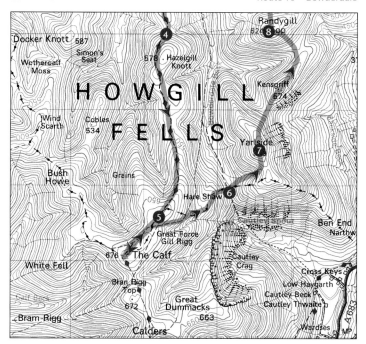

2. Run ahead, following the now grassy track. After 500 metres, the public bridleway turns L. Ignore this and continue to follow the grassy track as it climbs up the shoulder of West Fell. The angle eases as you reach the summit plateau. Run a short way across the undulating plateau to reach a high point at 541m 4.4km.

3. Descend slightly, before ascending again over a grassy hill. Bear R over the shoulder of the next hill and descend to the col beneath Hazelgill Knott 6.1km.

4. Bear R on a grassy track, climbing round the summit. Bear L as the ground flattens to meet the path from the summit. Descend slightly, before climbing the shoulder leading to **The Calf**. At the top of the shoulder, bear R on a flat path and run past a small tarn, before descending slightly to meet the bridleway at a larger tarn (on the R) 9km.

Yarlside's summit (photo: Hilary Moakes)

⑤ Turn R and run up the stony path to the trig point, which marks the summit of The Calf at 676m. Retrace the route back to the tarn and continue to run down the bridleway for approximately 500 metres. Turn R at a small stone culvert and take an intermittent path to Hare Shaw. Run across the tussocks, descending steeply to the col north of **Cautley Spout** waterfall. Cross the col to a path junction 11.5km.

⑥ Turn R up a small trod that climbs steeply to the R of the stream. Follow this until it joins the stream. Climb steeply up an intermittent path to reach a second col and path to the south of Yarlside's summit. Turn L and follow the path up the final steep section to the summit of **Yarlside** at 639m, marked by a small stone cairn 12.4km.

⑦ Run past the cairn, following a small grassy path. After 100 metres, bear R at a small peat scoop. Descend diagonally L, very, very steeply, to reach the col at the foot of **Kensgriff**. Take care to avoid the rocky gullies on the western slopes of Yarlside. Near the bottom, a faint path develops. Follow the path to the col. Climb steeply up the grassy path to the small stone cairn that marks the summit of Kensgriff. Run over the top and follow the path down towards

a small tarn. Bear L, following the path just below the tarn. At the path junction, continue straight ahead, climbing to the summit of **Randygill Top** at 624m. The path peters out just before the summit 14.4km.

8   From the summit, take the L path fork and descend gently at first, then more steeply, to the col at **Leathgill Bridge**. Continue ahead and climb steeply up the grassy track, to reach a broad ridge at spot height 586m. Run across the plateau, on an excellent track, to the far end and descend to a track junction 16.6km.

9   Take the L fork and run down the grassy track, passing a new section of fence and the remains of an old wall, to a track junction 18.3km.

10   Run down the stony track and through a couple of gates to meet the road. Turn L along the road back to the start 20km.

Route 17
Wild Boar Fell

Start/finish	Roadside parking on the Cumbria–North Yorkshire county border: SD 777 963
Distance	16.5km (10¼ miles)
Ascent	640m (2100ft)
Grade	Level 4
Time	2hr 30min
Terrain	A mixture of good tracks and paths, with some sections on small grassy paths across open moorland
Map	OS Landranger 98: Wensleydale & Upper Wharfedale
Refreshments	The Moorcock Inn, Garsdale Head; pubs, shops and cafés in Kirkby Stephen
Public transport	Bus 569 from Kirkby Stephen (limited service)

This is a run with a truly mountain feel. The route traverses remote Mallerstang in the north-west Yorkshire Dales and climbs the lonely Wild Boar Fell. The first section, which is relatively flat, follows the ancient Lady Anne's Highway past the sinuous limestone gorge of Hell Gill. The run then turns north through the Mallerstang valley, opposite the rocky and precipitous east face of Wild Boar Fell. The second section of the route, which takes in most of the ascent (500m), crosses under the famous Settle–Carlisle railway and then climbs the Pennine Bridleway up Wild Boar Fell's steep northern spur. A small path crosses the summit plateau to the trig point. The final section is a high-level run from the summit over Swarth Fell, finally dropping down across open fell to the start.

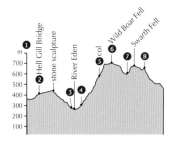

'Water Cut' sculpture, Mallerstang

1. Take the track that starts by the 'Welcome to Richmondshire' noticeboard down over the railway. Bear L and run along the track to a junction just before the river. Turn R up the track, crossing over the river. Continue to run up the track to a renovated farm. Run to the R of the farm, following the track up through the fields to **Hell Gill Bridge** 1.2km.

2. Turn L. Run along the flat grassy track as it contours north through the Mallerstang valley. After a couple of kilometres, you will reach a stone sculpture: the Water Cut, which matches the shape of the river valley beyond. Run down the grassy track, which changes to a stony track after a kilometre, crossing small streams to reach the road 5.2km.

3. Turn R along the road and then immediately L through the first gate. Run down the track and cross the infant **River Eden** by a stone bridge. Continue down the track for a few metres. Turn L over a small wooden bridge and take the footpath through the fields to the track to Hazel Gill Farm. Turn R to the farm 6.2km.

4. Bear L around the farm, then R up a grassy track, signposted 'Pennine Bridleway', to a gate. Run uphill and pass under the **Settle–Carlisle railway line**. Bear L, then R, following the track steeply upwards towards the open fell and past an old barn. Cross the stream to a gate. Turn L up the track. The gradient lessens after a few hundred metres as you reach a gate. Continue up the faint track, marked by a few way posts. Bear R at the foot of a steep bank and climb up to meet the wall at the col 8.25km.

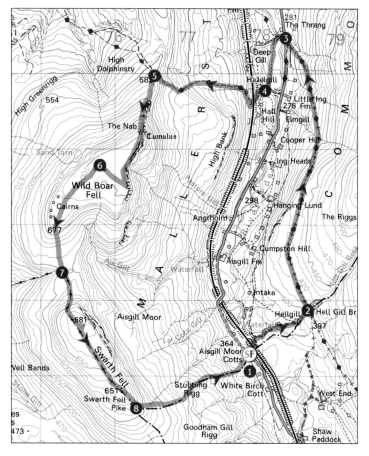

5 Turn L and run along the small grassy path up **The Nab**. The path passes through some old stone workings and past a small tarn before climbing steeply again to the summit plateau, marked by a cairn. Bear L and run along the small grassy path, which follows the escarpment edge, for a few hundred metres to reach a series of stone cairns and a shelter. Turn R, almost back on yourself, and run along a small grassy path, boggy in places, across the plateau to the summit trig point on **Wild Boar Fell** 10.6km.

The craggy, steep east face of Wild Boar Fell

Legend of the last boar

Legend has it that Wild Boar Fell gets its name from the last boar killed in England during the 15th century. It is more likely, however, that the name stems from the old Norse description of the mountain and its wild cliffs.

(6) Bear L, heading SW from the summit, and run down a faint grassy path. Pass through the faint remains of old mine workings. After approximately 300 metres, a fence appears on the L. Run parallel to the fence, along a path, to a stone cairn. Bear L to the fence and descend steeply down the fell, following a small path to the broad col between Wild Boar and Swarth Fell. Cross the col, following the fence to its junction with a wall 12.3km.

(7) Turn L over the fence and run past a small tarn on the L. Run alongside the wall, climbing up on to the broad summit of **Swarth Fell**, passing a small tarn on the L as you reach the plateau. Continue ahead before bearing L to the summit cairn. Return to the wall. Turn L. Run down the grassy path to a wall corner and fence junction. Run alongside the fence, descending to the col before climbing again to reach Swarth Fell Pike, marked by a small stone cairn 14.3km.

(8) Descend past a second cairn and then bear slightly L, heading NE down the pathless open fell, crossing the boggy headwaters of a small stream down to **Stubbing Rigg**. In good visibility, aim for the Hell's Gill wood on the opposite side of the valley. Pick up the quad bike track that crosses Stubbing Rigg and follow it downhill, back to the start 16.5km.

Route 18
Cautley Spout

Start/finish	Roadside parking by the A683: SD 698 969
Distance	17km (10½ miles)
Ascent	1110m (3640ft)
Grade	Level 4
Time	3hr
Terrain	Mainly grassy paths and tracks with short sections of stony paths
Map	OS Landranger 98: Wensleydale & Upper Wharfedale; OS Landranger 97: Kendal & Morecambe
Refreshments	Cross Keys Temperance Bar at the start; pubs, cafés and shops in Kirkby Stephen and Sedbergh
Public transport	Bus S2 from Sedbergh

This high-level route takes in the higher hills of the Howgills and the magnificent Cautley Spout waterfall. The run combines broad grassy ridges with steep ascents and descents. Beginning with a gentle run alongside the River Rawthey, the route then turns north-west and climbs steeply alongside Cautley Spout waterfall and under the magnificent Cautley Crag. A short steep climb brings you to the grassy plateau of Great Dummacks and Calders. The second section crosses Arant Haw, before a long steep grassy descent leads to the western edge of the Howgills. The final section involves a 400-metre climb to the highest hills in the Howgills: Bram Rigg Top, followed by a short out-and-back run to The Calf. The climb is long, but has stunning views of the steep-sided western Howgills. The run finally descends a small path, leading back to the outward route at the top of Cautley Spout.

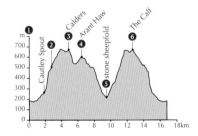

Safety

In poor visibility, this run is a serious one, requiring high levels of navigation and route-finding. Consider using a 1:25000 scale map (OS Explorer OL19: Howgill Fells & Upper Eden Valley) in these conditions. The steep nature of the grassy ascents and descents makes studded fell shoes a must.

Did you know?

The Cross Keys Temperance Bar was bequeathed to the National Trust in 1949 on the condition it was used as an unlicensed inn. The building was most likely a farm, originally, dating back to the 1600s.

1. From the Cross Keys Temperance Bar, cross the River Rawthey by a small wooden bridge, signposted 'Cautley Spout'. Turn L and run alongside the river for 500 metres. Bear R and follow the path to the foot of **Cautley Spout** waterfall. Climb the steep grassy path to a junction. Bear L and continue to climb; the path soon becomes paved. Follow this up to the top. Turn L and run along a small rocky path around into a stream gully. Run ahead to reach a second stream 2.5km.

2. Cross the stream and climb a small grassy path, heading S, up on to the edge of Cautley Crag. Climb steeply towards the summit plateau of **Great Dummacks**. Run along the small path around the edge of the escarpment, before turning sharp R, taking a small path over the grassy top. Run along the path as it descends to a track junction. Bear R and climb up to a fence. Run alongside the fence to a corner, before climbing to **Calders'** summit cairn 4.8km.

Cautley Spout waterfall

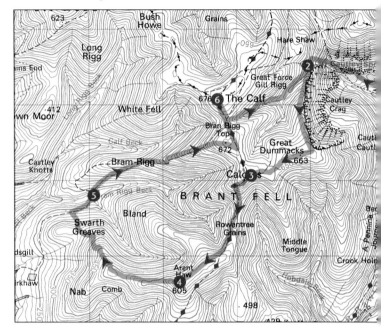

Descending the grassy slopes of Arant Haw

3 Bear L from the cairn and run down the path, following the fence to the col. Follow the path up and over the small shoulder, descending again, before climbing up to a path junction and marker post. Bear R and run along the grassy path to **Arant Haw**, marked by a stone cairn 6.8km.

4 Bear R, heading W, from the cairn and run down a small grassy path that leads down the ridge to a small knoll. Continue to descend. At the first path junction, bear L and then a few metres later bear R on a quad bike path leading to a second knoll, marked by a small pile of stones. Bear R, picking up a quad bike path that leads steeply down to a rusty sheep fold at the col. Run ahead, past the sheepfold, for approximately 20 metres. Turn R down a quad bike track. Follow this to the stony track. Turn R and run down the track, crossing a small stream to a large stone sheepfold 9.4km.

5 Continue ahead, crossing a second stream, and run up the track. After 50 metres, bear R and climb the steep grassy track to **Bram Rigg**. After 1km, the ridge is reached. Bear R, climbing steeply past a sheepfold, to reach a footpath and quad bike track junction. Continue ahead, climbing steeply up and over Bram Rigg Top. Run along the grassy track, descending slightly to reach a stony track. Turn L and run along the track, descending to a col, before climbing to **The Calf** trig point 12.6km.

6 Retrace the route back down to the col. Turn L and run down a small path, alongside the start of a small stream. After a short distance, it widens into a stream gully. Run down the path, which is steep and rocky in places, past a stream junction and stone sheepfold, to rejoin the outward route at waypoint 2. Follow the outward route back to the top of **Cautley Spout** and descend back to the start 17km.

Route 19
Pendragon Castle to Skipton Castle Ultra
Leg 1 (Pendragon Castle to Hawes)

Start	Pendragon Castle: NY 781 025.
Finish	Hawes Youth Hostel: SD 867 897
Distance	21.5km (13½ miles)
Ascent	415m (1360ft)
Grade	Level 1
Time	3hr
Terrain	A mixture of fields, woodland and grassy paths and tracks
Map	OS Landranger 98: Wensleydale & Upper Wharfedale
Refreshments	Shops, pubs and cafés in Hawes
Public transport	Train to Kirby Stephen. Buses S4 from Sedbergh and 569 from Kirkby Stephen (limited summer service) are the closest

This is a fantastic run that traverses high above the remote valleys of Mallerstang and upper Wensleydale. Starting at the ruined Pendragon Castle, the first section of the route runs through fields and woodland alongside the River Eden, before climbing up to a stone sculpture above the Mallerstang valley. The second section follows Lady Anne's Way along the eastern side of the valley, passing old abandoned farms and crossing into the upper reaches of Wensleydale. The running is excellent: a gently undulating grassy path with excellent views of the northern Dales. The final section begins with a short descent into the valley, before continuing along good paths and tracks through farmland to Appersett. A short section of road follows, before a final short section through farmland leads to Hawes. The whole route has few navigational difficulties.

Uther's legendary abode

Pendragon Castle was the legendary castle of Uther Pendragon, father of King Arthur. The present Norman castle was built in the 12th century.

---

1 Run back to the road from the castle. Turn L and run down the road for a couple of hundred metres to cross the **River Eden**. Turn L, signposted 'Shoregill', and run along the footpath (Lady Anne's Way) through the field to a small footbridge.

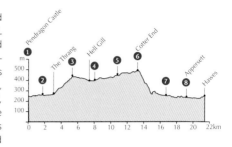

Cross the bridge and climb up into the field. Bear R at the far end to the stile. Turn L and follow the path through several more fields, running parallel to the river, to reach the farm at **Shoregill**. Turn L past Shoregill House and descend the track to the river bridge 1.9km.

2 Turn R, following a small footpath through the wood to a tarmac farm track. Turn R and run through to the end of the farm buildings. Bear R and follow the path through the fields, running alongside the river once more.

Waterfall

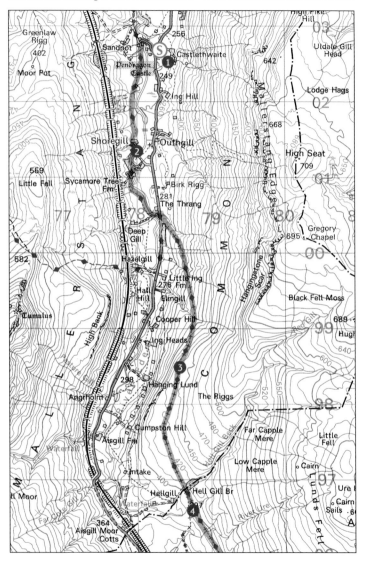

Steam train on the Settle–Carlisle line with Whernside in the background

Continue ahead to reach a small stone bridge. Turn L and follow the track up to the road, just south of **The Thrang**. Turn R and run down the road for a few metres. Take a track on the L, signposted 'Pennine Bridleway – Hell Gill'. Follow the stony track for a couple of kilometres, as it climbs up on to the side of **Mallerstang**, to reach a stone sculpture called the 'Water Cut', which stands high above the River Eden 5.3km.

3   Run along the grassy track as it gradually descends to a small patch of woodland and the impressive limestone gorge of **Hell Gill**. Pass through the gate and run down the track for a few hundred metres to reach a track junction 7.4km.

4   Bear L and run along the grassy track as it gradually climbs towards the ruined farm of **High Hall**. Run past the ruin and follow the track as it crosses several small streams and ruined stone barns to reach a short uphill section on a pitched stone path that leads to the ruin of High Dyke 10km.

5   Run along the grassy path as it contours around the side of Mallerstang, before turning SW towards Hawes, heading in the direction of Thwaite Bridge Common. Continue ahead at the path/track junction, signposted

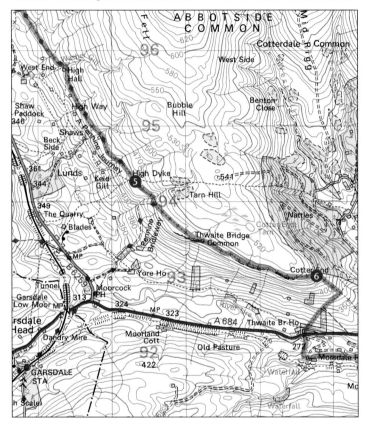

'Cotter End', climbing up on to the escarpment edge. At the far end, the path descends steeply, past an ancient lime kiln, to reach a wall and gate 13.7km.

6 Pass through the gate and run down the grassy path for 400 metres to a path junction. Turn R and descend across rough pasture to the corner of a small wood, marked by a wooden ladder stile. Continue to descend to the wood, aiming for a ladder stile to the L of the farm. Follow the small stony path down through the wood to the road at Thwaite Bridge Cottage. Take

care crossing the busy **A684** and run up the footpath directly opposite. Follow the small path around the outside of the wall to meet a farm track. Turn L through the gate and run down over the river into the farmyard. Follow the footpath around the back of the farm and run through the fields alongside the river to reach a small wooden gate. Pass through the gate and cross a narrow, wooded boggy field to reach a track 16.6km.

7 Turn L and run along the good track through a small valley. Descend past **Birkrigg Farm**. Turn R at a track bend and run through the field to a small stream. Cross the stream and climb up through the wood. Turn L and follow the grassy path through the fields. Descend back down to the river and run along the path to meet the A684 at a bridge 19km.

8 Turn R and follow a small path into **Appersett**. Follow the road over the river and through the village. Run along the road for approximately 1km. Turn L and run along the footpath through the fields. At the footpath junction, continue straight ahead and then bear R up into **Hawes**. Turn R and follow the road to the Youth Hostel 21.5km.

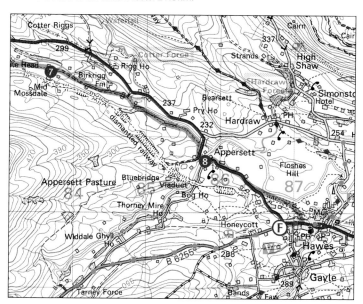

THE NORTH-EAST DALES, SWALEDALE AND WENSLEYDALE

Running along the Pennine Way towards the Tan Hill Inn (Route 27)

Route 20
Aysgarth

Start	National Park Visitor Centre, Aysgarth: SE 011 887
Distance	18km (11¼ miles)
Ascent	315m (1030ft)
Grade	Level 1
Time	2hr 30min
Terrain	A mixture of grassy and stone paths and tracks with half a mile of road leading up to Castle Bolton, the only steep part of the run
Map	OS Landranger 98: Wensleydale & Upper Wharfedale
Refreshments	National Park Visitor Centre; pubs and cafés in Aysgarth
Public transport	Bus 856 and 156 from Hawes/Leyburn; bus 875 from Grassington

This is a low-level, relatively flat run that starts and finishes at Aysgarth Falls, one of the Dale's most popular attractions. Aysgarth Falls, formed where the River Ure flows over a series of limestone steps, is particularly impressive after heavy rain. There are three sets of falls; the run starts by passing the lower and middle falls and finishes past the impressive upper falls.

The first section of the run is through scenic woods and over fields to the impressive 14th-century Castle Bolton, which dominates this area of Wensleydale. The second section turns west, following a track high up on the shoulder of Wensleydale, through an old lead mine to the hamlet of Woodhall. The last section follows the River Ure east through fields back to the falls. The run can be completed in either direction and is a good alternative on a poor weather day. In the spring, the sound of curlews, oystercatchers and lapwings, to name a few, make the run fantastic.

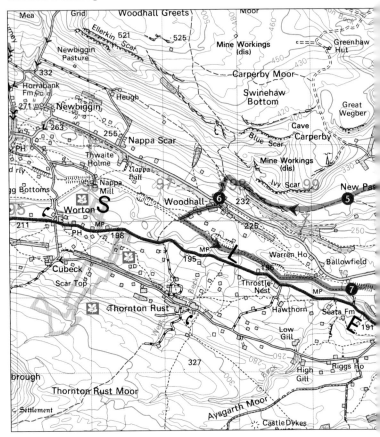

1 From the car park, follow the signs to **Aysgarth Falls**. Cross the road into Freeholders Wood. Turn R, signposted 'Castle Bolton', and follow the path to a gate. Run ahead. After 100 metres, take a small path on the L. Run along the path, following the fence line, and through the fields up to a farm. Bear L on the track through the farm. Turn R and run along the footpath through the fields to reach a wall and path junction. Turn R in front of the wall. Follow the path to the gate. Run ahead to meet a grassy track 2.2km.

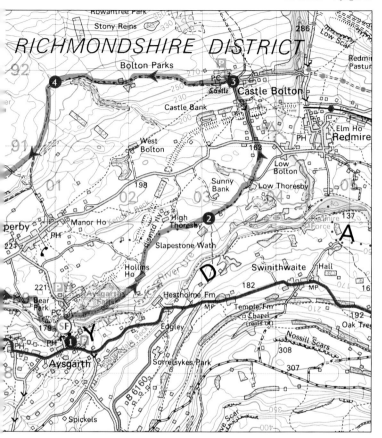

2 Run along the grassy track, through the gate into a wooded lane. Follow the lane to a farm. Pass in front of the farm and follow the track for 50 metres. Turn L on a footpath through fields, signposted 'Castle Bolton'. Run across the fields to the road. Cross the road and run up the road to **Castle Bolton** 4.9km.

3 Run around the castle to the car park. Continue ahead on the track signposted 'Askrigg'. Run past a corrugated-metal barn. Bear R and uphill on the track. Follow this to the farm buildings and gate. Continue along the wall. Turn L through the gate and bear R down over a small stream and up to another gate. Turn L through the gate. Run along the grassy track to a bridge and ford 7.6km.

4 Continue ahead through a gate. Bear L on grassy track, signposted 'Askrigg and Caperby'. Follow the track downhill and contour to a wall junction. Run ahead uphill, signposted 'Askrigg'. Run through several fields. Continue straight on at the track fork, before descending to a gate in the wall, just past the obvious **communications mast** above on the hillside 10.1km.

Aysgarth Falls is one of the Yorkshire Dales' most visited attractions

Castle Bolton rising above Wensleydale

(5) Run down the excellent grassy path to the old lead mine. Follow the grassy track around the L edge of the old workings to a stony track. Run ahead to a ford and bridge. Cross the bridge and turn L, following the track through a gate and short section of walled lane to a track junction. Turn L, signposted 'Woodhall'. Follow the track to the road 12.2km.

(6) Cross the road and run down the lane to **Woodhall**. Ignore the footpath sign on the L and continue to follow the road, which becomes a track, down to the disued railway. Turn L over a stile and run along the bottom of the railway embankment, through the fields, to reach the **River Ure**. Follow the path through the fields between the river and the old railway for a couple of kilometres to reach a track just upstream from a bridge 15.5km.

(7) Cross the track and bear L through a small gate to rejoin the old railway line at a bridge. Ascend on to the railway line. Turn R and follow this to a wall corner. Turn L through the fields and then R uphill, back towards the railway line. Turn L through the fields to a large farm (**Dear Park**). Cross the farm track and climb up stone steps into the field. Follow the path around the tennis court. Run ahead, following footpath signs, through the fields back to the old railway. Turn L through the woods and run down to Aysgarth Falls. Follow the path to the road and up to the National Park Visitor Centre 18km.

Route 21
Thornton Rust

Start	Small car park at Thornton Rust: SD 972 888
Distance	15km (9½ miles)
Ascent	410m (1350ft)
Grade	Level 2
Time	2hr
Terrain	The run mainly follows good tracks with shorter sections of moorland tracks and paths, which may be boggy at times during the year
Map	OS Landranger 98: Wensleydale & Upper Wharfedale
Refreshments	Pubs and shops in Aysgarth and Bainbridge
Public transport	Bus 156 from Hawes/Leyburn

This is a good circular route, with not too much ascent or descent, that follows ancient tracks high above Wensleydale and Bishopdale. The run starts from the small hamlet of Thornton Rust, just off the A684. The run is best done in the spring, when the moors are alive with birds like the lapwing, curlew and golden plover. The route passes close to ancient settlements, cairns and henges, which are worth a visit.

1 From the car park cross the small ford and run along the track up out of Thornton Rust. Follow the walled lane as it zigzags up on to the moor. Continue past an old stone barn to a gate and small ford. Continue for 100 metres to the end of the lane 0.9km.

> ### Thor's old digs
> In 1066, the manor that became Thornton Rust belonged to 'Thor'.

2 Turn L, signposted 'bridleway', up the grassy path, across rough pasture-land, to a gate. Bear R, then L on a grassy, sometimes boggy, path that zigzags across the undulating moor. Descend to a small stream, then climb to a ladder stile and gate. Continue for another 100 metres to a path and track junction 2.3km.

Old stone trough, Carpley Green

③ Bear L and run along the small grassy spur. Turn R through a gate. Turn immediately L and run to a second gate. Climb gradually upwards on the grassy track through several fields to an old stone drinking trough. Run down the small path, bearing L through the fields to the small road at **Carpley Green** 3.9km.

④ Turn L along the road through the farm. Run up the old walled lane (Busk Lane) from the farm. The lane steepens as it climbs up through **Stake Allotments**. The gradient lessens as it passes some sheep pens. Continue to run up the track to the top of Stake Moor. The track levels off as it reaches the summit. Run past a small stone cairn on the L to a track and path junction 6.9km.

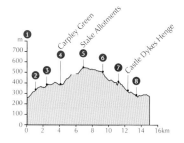

⑤ Turn sharp L, signposted 'Bridleway Thoralby'. Follow the small grassy path back past the stone cairn to meet a second

133

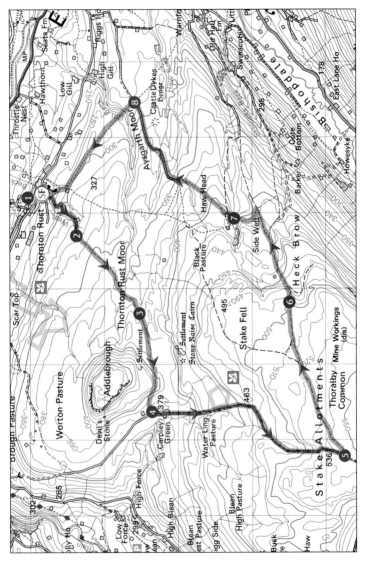

Heathery tracks through Aysgarth Moor

track coming in from the L. Bear R and run along the grassy track, which soon becomes rocky. Continue ahead at the next junction and run for approximately 1km to another track junction. Take the L fork and run downhill on the grassy track, which rejoins the stony track after a few hundred metres 9.3km.

6 Turn L and run down the stony track, through a short walled lane section and across the ford at the bottom. Run along the track to a junction. Take the L fork up and around the small hill to a gate across the track. Turn L 100 metres before the gate on to a small footpath, marked by stone cairn. Run along the path to a gate. Run down the steep path crossing the footbridge over the small stream. Climb steeply up to the wall 11.1km.

7 Bear R, signposted 'Aysgarth'. Run across the moor, following a grassy track, and descend to a gate. Turn R. Cross the small stream to reach a path and track junction. Pass through the gate and run down the wide walled track to the ford. Continue ahead, passing to the L of **Castle Dykes Henge**, to reach a footpath and track junction 13.3km.

8 Turn L, signposted 'Thornton Rust', and run along the path through the field. Descend steeply over a small stream and climb up the opposite bank. Bear R to a stile. Run through the fields, following yellow-topped marker posts, towards Thornton Rust. Bear R to drop back to the track. Turn R into **Thornton Rust** 15km.

Route 22
Bainbridge

Start	Roadside parking by Bainbridge village green: SD 933 901
Distance	22.5km (14 miles)
Ascent	840m (2760ft)
Grade	Level 3
Time	3.5hr
Terrain	A mixture of good tracks and small footpaths that can be boggy at times
Map	OS Landranger 98: Wensleydale & Upper Wharfedale
Refreshments	Café, shops and pub in Bainbridge
Public transport	Buses 156 and 856 from Leyburn/Hawes; bus 875 from Grassington/Hawes

This is a long, tough route that covers a wide range of terrain. The run begins with a straightforward trail run up the Roman Road from Bainbridge, which climbs high into the hills. A short road section is followed by a fast fell run down grassy paths, through Bardale to the hamlet of Marsett. The final section runs along stony tracks and grassy paths through Stalling Busk and round Semerwater, a large glacial lake, back to the start.

Safety

The middle section contains tricky navigation through farmland that may be impassable after very heavy rain.

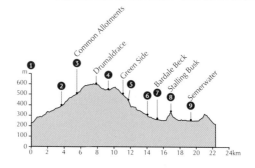

1 Run up the small road to the R of the village green, past the old temperance hall. Bear R up and out of Bainbridge. After three-quarters of a kilometre, the road levels. Continue ahead until the road turns L. Run straight up the stony track (**Roman Road**), signposted 'Beggarman's Road', to a road crossing 3.5km.

2 Cross the road and climb up the steepening track. After 500 metres, the track zigzags over a small stream. Continue ahead, past a footpath crossing. Continue to run up towards **Common Allotments** and a second footpath crossing 5.8km.

3 Continue to run up the track as it reaches the Wether Fell and **Drumaldrace** plateau. The track now crosses limestone bedding planes, and the walls are full of tiny fossils. Most of the day's ascent has been done. Run along the track as it contours around to the south of Drumaldrace, before dropping gently down to meet the road up from Hawes 9.1km.

4 Bear L along the road to a junction. Turn L, signposted 'Kettlewell'. After a few metres, take the footpath on the L through the field, signposted 'Marsett'. Follow the path, as it curves beneath a grassy knoll, down to a flatter boggy section. Pick up a small path bearing R to a slight corner in the wall. Bear L along the wall and run down the grassy path over **Bardale Head** and past **Green Side** to a small group of trees 11.4km.

Looking east across to the flat summit of Addleborough

⑤ Turn R through the gate and run diagonally L, on a small quad bike track, down the grassy spur to a gate. Continue steeply down to cross a small stream, up through the gate and over a small rise, to reach a broken wall and marker post. Bear sharp L on a faint path to a gate. Turn R before the gate and follow a faint path through the field, down across the stream to a corrugated-iron-roofed shelter. Pass through the wall and follow the quad bike track that runs parallel to a wall, gradually losing height. After approximately 1km, bear R on a small path to a stile in the wall (near a fenced section) just above the river 14km.

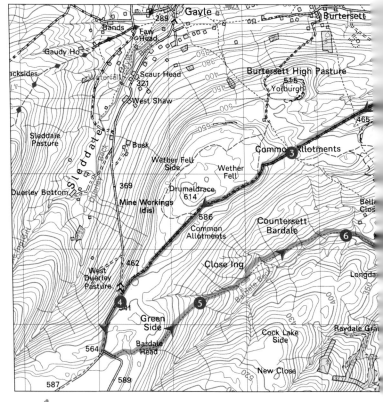

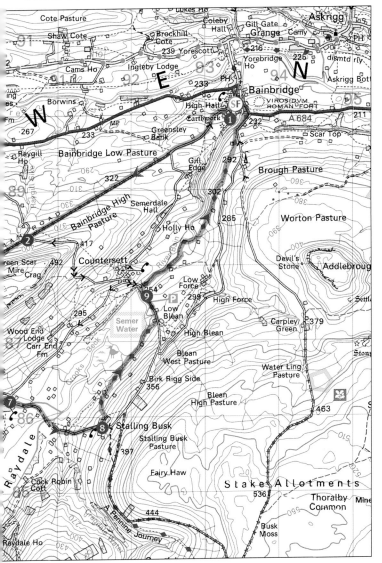

Limestone scenery above Wensleydale

6   Run down the small grassy path to a wall. Bear L through the fields along the wall into coppiced hazel woodland. Continue to follow the path to reach a farm. Pass in front of the farm via a small riverside path on the R to reach a track. Turn R to the road bridge over **Bardale Beck** 15.1km.

7   Cross the beck. Turn L at the telephone box. Run along the track, signposted 'Stalling Busk', to the footbridge. Cross the river and continue a short distance to a second river. Do not cross the river, but take a small path on the R to reach a track. Continue ahead to cross the river via the ford. Run up the steep, rocky track to the road at **Stalling Busk** 16.8km.

8   Turn L along the road and then L down a small footpath, signposted 'Ruined Church'. Run down the path, bearing R at the ruined church, through the fields around **Semerwater**. The small path is good to begin with, but crosses boggy fields to reach a road. Turn L along the road to the Semerwater car park 19km.

9   Run along the road a short distance to the **River Bain**. Turn R on a footpath, signposted 'Bainbridge', that follows the river bank. After approximately half a kilometre, the path leaves the river and climbs steeply up through the fields above the river gorge. Run down the grassy path, parallel to the road, to a stile. Turn L down the road over the River Bain back to the start 22.5km.

> **Short fame for Bain**
>
> The River Bain is, at just less than 4km in length, one of England's shortest, named rivers.

Route 23
Maiden Castle (Reeth)

Start	Small car park: SE 020 982
Distance	18.5km (11½ miles)
Ascent	740m (2430ft)
Grade	Level 2
Time	2.5hr
Terrain	Mainly good tracks with a few sections of grassy paths
Map	OS Landranger 98: Wensleydale & Upper Wharfedale
Refreshments	Shops, pubs and cafés in Reeth
Public transport	Bus 830 from Hawes/Ingleton; bus 30 from Richmond is the closest

This is a Wizard of Oz route; substitute a wide runnable track for the yellow brick road and you get the idea. This is an easy run to navigate, as it follows a track for 16km. The only tricky section is the last 2km. The first section of the run uses a new track (not all of which is marked on older versions of the 1:50000 map) to climb high on to the moor. The middle section descends gently through the mine workings of Apedale and up over Greets Hill. The final section includes a 'sting in the tail' ascent of Long Scar, possibly a Bronze Age fortification. Then a fast descent along a small bridleway completes the route at the Iron Age Maiden Castle.

Running through the ages

The run takes in the old lead mining ruins that are a feature of this part of the Dales and visits Long Scar, which possibly dates back to the Bronze Age, as well as the Iron Age Maiden Castle.

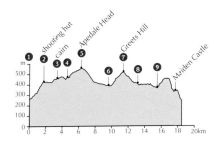

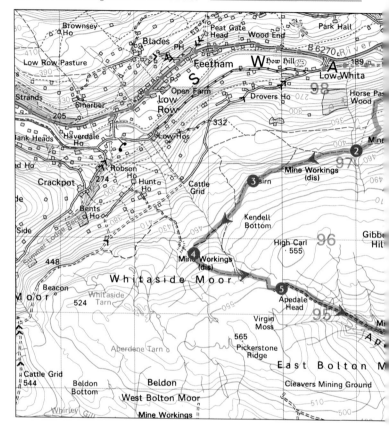

① Leave the car park and take a good track gently uphill, signposted 'Castle Bolton'. The track soon steepens as it zigzags up the hillside to a track junction. Turn R and follow the track to the large shooting hut 1.8km.

② Run along the track as it crosses a stream and levels off before descending and climbing again steeply around the top of the **old mine workings**. Run along the shoulder of the hill, aiming for a stone cairn. Turn R off the track and follow a grassy track to the **cairn** 3.5km.

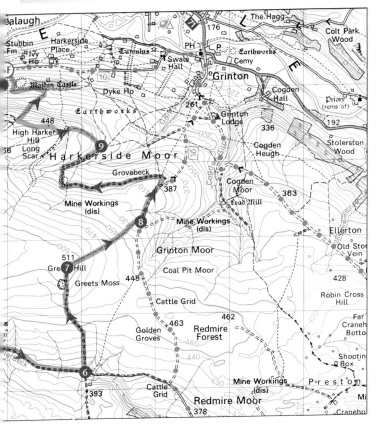

3. Bear R back up to the stone track and turn R. Run past a small bridleway, marked by a cairn. This is the bridleway marked on the map. Continue over a small stream and up to a substantial area of ruined mine workings and a track junction 4.8km.

4. Turn L and run up the steep track, alongside a small gully, towards the top of the moor. Cross the plateau, passing piles of stones, to a small cairn. Turn R at the cairn and through a gate to reach **Apedale Head**, the highest point of the day, marked by a cairn 6.4km.

The ramparts of Maiden Castle, an Iron Age fort

5 Run down the track, which is gentle at first but then followed by a short steeper section through mine workings and spoil heaps, into **Apedale**. Bear R at the track junction and continue to run down the track to a large area of **mine workings**. Continue ahead to reach a track crossroads, marked by a small stone building with a larger metal shelter 9.9km.

6 Turn L and run up the bridleway, through a band of shooting butts, towards the summit of **Greets Hill**. Bear R at the junction and follow the track past the small quarry to the summit cairn 11.4km.

7 Bear R from the cairn, through a gate and run down a small muddy path through the heather to another cairn. Continue to descend the grassy, sometimes rocky, path to the road. Turn L at the road and follow it for 500 metres. Turn L and follow the small bridleway a short distance to the track 13.3km.

8 Turn L and run up the track to more **mine workings**. Follow the track past the old mine building and down past a large spoil heap. Continue to run down the track, over a stream, down to the junction of several tracks 15.6km.

Shooting hut at the entrance to Apedale

9. Turn L and follow the track steeply uphill to the north-east end of the lime-stone embankment of Long Scar. Pass through the scar to a track junction marked with a signpost. Turn R on a grassy track through the heather, past a couple of cairns, to meet the bridleway that descends from the mine workings on **High Harker Hill**. This is marked by collection of small boulders. Turn R down the grassy shallow gully and then descend the small steep bridleway to a footpath. Turn L along the path through the heather for a few hundred metres to a stone cairn. Turn R just before the cairn and run down to the western ramparts of **Maiden Castle**. Follow the small grassy path down to the start 18.5km.

Route 24
Gunnerside Gill

Start/finish	Small car park at Gunnerside: SD 950 982
Distance	15km (9¼ miles)
Ascent	575m (1890ft)
Grade	Level 4.
Time	2.5hr
Terrain	A mixture of woodland paths, stone tracks and small grassy paths
Map	OS Landranger 98: Wensleydale & Upper Wharfedale; OS Landranger 92: Barnard Castle & Richmond
Refreshments	The King's Head pub and Ghyllfoot tea room in Gunnerside
Public transport	Bus 830 from Hawes/Ingleton; bus 30 from Richmond

This is a wonderful run full of geological and mining interest. The route follows the course of the magnificent Gunnerside Gill, passing through a rich lead mining heritage of old mine buildings and ancient mines. The second section of the route climbs up and out of Gunnerside to cross high moorland, before descending to more mine workings. This is followed by a grassy traverse high above upper Swaledale, which involves running along small paths on steep hillsides, creating an exposed and airy run with some difficult navigation in poor weather. The final section is through hay meadows, rich in plant life, following the River Swale downstream back to the start.

1 From the car park, turn L over the bridge and then L alongside **Gunnerside Gill**. Run up the path, following it round an old house and through the fields back to the river. Run upstream, following the small footpath, through the woods, high above the river. At the far end of the wood, descend to a wooden bridge over a small stream. Pass through the gate and run along the wall side to the old mine workings 2km.

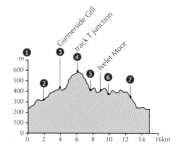

146

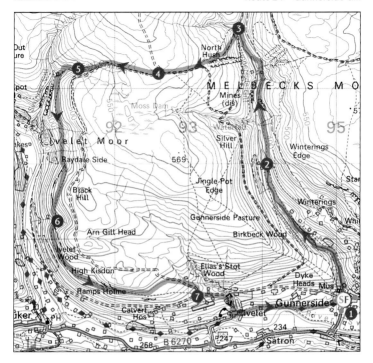

> **Did you know?**
>
> Gunnerside Gill lead mines and ore works are listed under the Ancient Monuments and Archaeological Areas Act as representing an exceptionally well-preserved lead mining area. The lead mines date back to the 17th century, although earlier workings have been found.

② Follow the path upstream to cross a stile. Bear R up the path and alongside the wall. Cross through the wall, opposite a ruined mine. Run uphill along the path to the junction with a bridleway, marked by a cairn. Continue ahead. The path contours through the upper part of the gill to a large collection of **mine workings**. Run a short distance past the mine workings to a footpath and bridleway junction, fingerpost and cairn. Turn L and run down the path to another set of mine buildings and a stone slab bridge over Gunnerside Gill 4.5km.

3 Cross the bridge and turn L (downstream). Run down the track for 50 metres and then turn R on to a small path that climbs up and out of the valley. The path becomes steeper and zigzags past a stone cairn at the bottom of a steep bank. Climb the steep bank and run across flatter moorland, past stone cairns, to a small old mine. Run along the path to meet a recently made, larger stone track. Bear R along the track, signposted 'C to C', to a track T junction 6km.

4 Run down the track for a few hundred metres, then turn R on to a paved footpath that descends into a stream gully. The path becomes rockier and steeper, dropping down to two old ruined mine buildings 7.7km.

5 Turn L, crossing a small stream just before the buildings, and climb out of the gully. The path rises gradually and then traverses the grassy ledge of **Ivelet Moor**, under rocky outcrops. Descend a grassy bank to a wall crossing. Bear L after the stile, across a small boulder field and around the base of some cliffs. Follow the path around the head of a small stream and then

Footbridge leaving the woodland section leading to Gunnerside Gill

Remains of the old lead mines in Gunnerside Gill

alongside a ruined stone wall. Continue on the path, crossing two more stream heads to a footpath junction and waymarker post. DO NOT descend into the gully, which has a rocky step at the bottom. Instead, bear L steeply uphill and around the top of the gill. Follow the small, exposed grassy path along the hillside. After three-quarters of a kilometre, bear R and descend steeply, following way posts to a stream 9.9km.

6 Cross the stream and run along the gradually descending path high above the valley to rejoin the ruined wall. Follow the path as the hillside opens up. Bear L to meet the track that descends from Black Hill. Turn R and follow the track a short way to the road 12.7km.

7 Turn L along the road for a few hundred metres to a T junction. Turn R and descend the steep road to the hamlet of **Ivelet**. Turn L at the telephone box and pass through the farm buildings, signposted 'Gunnerside'. Bear R down the footpath to cross a stream and up to a stone barn. Follow the footpath through the fields back to the start 15km.

Route 25
Muker

Start/finish	Public car park at Muker: SD 910 978
Distance	9km (5½ miles)
Ascent	400m (1310ft)
Grade	Level 2
Time	1.5hr
Terrain	A mixture of farm lanes, grassy tracks, small grassy/rocky paths and stony tracks
Map	OS Landranger 98: Wensleydale & Upper Wharfedale; OS Landranger 91: Appleby-in-Westmorland
Refreshments	Pubs, shops, campsites and toilets in Muker
Public transport	Bus 830 from Hawes/Ingleton; bus 30 from Richmond

Muker is located high up in the northern dale of Swaledale, surrounded by flower-rich grasslands and fields, complete with stone barns. Swaledale is a large glaciated valley that was inhabited long before the Vikings established the village of Mjor akr. The village grew rich in the eighteenth and nineteenth centuries from lead that was mined from the surrounding fells, before being carried along ancient drove roads. Today Muker is a popular tourist destination.

The route, which is a short one, circuits Kisdon Hill, following sections of the Pennine Way and the old Corpse Road. Before the church was built, corpses had to be carried from higher up the dale to the church at Grinton. The first and last sections of the run follow the same route along an old farm track out of the village. They are linked by an excellent grassy traverse high above the River Swale, which provides views across to old lead mines. The final section crosses grassy fields to the north-west of Kisdon, before turning south, following a track up and over the shoulder of Kisdon to meet the outward route.

> ### Did you know?
> The River Swale is a fast-flowing river. Its name comes from the Anglo Saxon 'Sualuae' meaning rapid and liable to deluge.

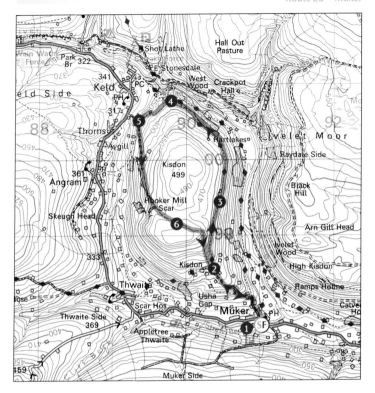

1 Turn L out of the car park and cross over the river. Turn L and run alongside the **River Swale** for a short distance. Take the first R turn uphill past the Literary Institute and village hall. Bear L to Grange Farm. Take the R fork, then bear L, signposted 'Keld'. Run up the walled lane, past the Old Vicarage to a gate. Continue ahead as the track zigzags up above Swaledale, bearing L. Continue straight on along a grassy track, signposted 'Keld' 1.3km.

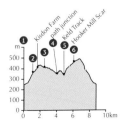

Classic limestone scenery

2 Run along a walled lane, through the gate to the farm at **Kisdon**. Just past the farm, bear diagonally R across the field, signposted 'Pennine Way Keld', to a wall. Turn L, signposted 'Pennine Way. Ignore the grassy track on the L. Instead, follow the wall to a gate. Run along the grassy path next to the wall as it crosses a small patch of scree. Descend gradually, passing over two old stone walls to a gate. Cross the field to a small gate in the wall corner 2.5km.

3 Continue to contour around the hillside, below the limestone escarpment, to reach a ruined shooting lodge. Descend gradually on the rocky path alongside a ruined wall. The path bears L, following the course of the valley NW above the woodland. Run above the woodland for approximately 1km. The path rises to a path junction and signpost overlooking a large limestone cliff 4.1km.

4 Bear L up the footpath and run around the north side of Kisdon, overlooking the hamlet of Keld. Continue to run along the grassy footpath to a gate. Turn L in front of the gate to reach a small gate with a wooden post and footpath marker sign. Go through the gate and run along the wall side to a short section of walled lane. Run past the stone barn to a fence wall junction (NY 894 006). Bear L through the gate and descend along the track to meet the Keld track at a junction 4.8km.

Path to the east of Kisdon

⑤ Turn L and run steeply uphill on the stone track to a gate. Continue ahead to a second gate and farmhouse on the L. As the track turns L to the farm, continue ahead on the grassy track. Run along the grassy track through the fields, crossing **Hooker Mill Scar**, to a gate and signpost 6.1km.

⑥ Run through the next field, signposted 'Muker', along a ruined walled lane and across the broad top of the hill to a wall corner and gate. Descend across the field gently at first and then more steeply. At the end of the field, turn R down into a walled lane. Follow this steeply down to the farmhouse passed on the outward leg of the journey. Run down the track back into **Muker** and the start 9km.

Route 26
Great Shunner Fell

Start	Track/road junction, Thwaite: SD 889 983
Finish	Track/road junction, Hardraw: SD 866 912
Distance	13km (8 miles)
Ascent	630m (2070ft)
Descent	717m (1975ft)
Grade	Level 2
Time	2hr
Terrain	As the route follows a national trail, the going is generally excellent and the navigation straightforward. A stony track leads from the start, followed by paved sections and grassy paths to the summit. The descent follows a stony path with sections of paving and grass
Map	OS Landranger 98: Wensleydale & Upper Wharfedale
Refreshments	Pub and café in Hardraw; café in Thwaite
Public transport	Bus 830 from Hawes; bus 30 from Richmond

This is a great arc of a run that crosses Great Shunner Fell from north to south, following the Pennine Way. The route is a linear one, and the logistics of getting from the start to the finish need to be considered. The best way is to park a car at Hadraw and cycle the 10km up and over the Buttertubs pass, the route of the 2014 Tour de France, to Thwaite. Run over the tops, then return by car to pick up the bike.

The first section follows a walled track from the start, climbing up and out of the valley. This then changes to a path following the flat ground north of Great Shunner Fell. The second section turns south-west and climbs to the summit via Bleaberry Head, past a stone beacon. The final section, from the summit, follows the Pennine Way south, descending in a series of steps punctuated by flatter sections over Black Hill Moss, before dropping down the walled track into Hardraw.

Butter stores and bicycle cheer

The Buttertubs are deep limestone clefts reputedly used to store butter in the summer. During the 2014 Tour de France, the pass was lined with thousands of spectators as one of the world's toughest cycle races came to Yorkshire.

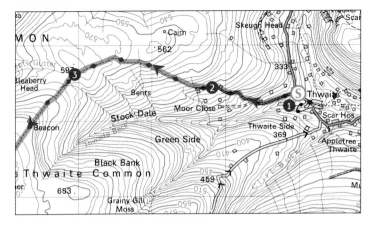

1. Run along the walled track, signposted 'Pennine Way Hardraw'. The rocky track climbs steadily for the first kilometre, before levelling off to reach a gate 1.4km.

2. Continue ahead, following the track uphill. After a few hundred metres, the track changes to a paved path, heading for the flat ground of **Bleaberry Head**. Run past an old mine working on the L, before climbing, passing occasional cairns, to a high point, marked by a cairn at **597m** 3.1km.

3. Descend a grassy path for 100 metres, before climbing steeply on a paved path to a large cairn, marked on the map as a beacon. Run ahead, past a small tarn on the L, to the summit of **Great Shunner Fell** at 716m. The trig point is

Running along the track as it climbs out of Thwaite

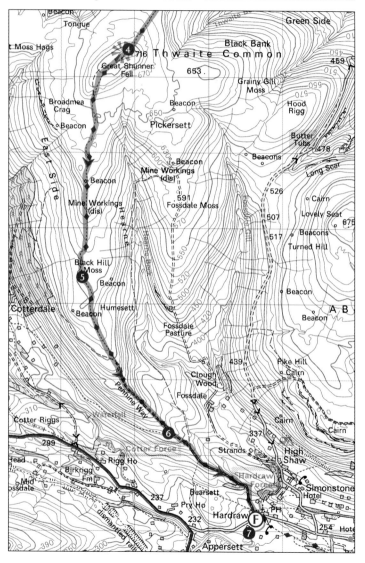

A snowy Great Shunner Fell

incorporated into the cross-shaped stone shelter that marks the summit 4.9km.

④ Run S down the path to a fence. Continue descending, following a stony path towards Hawes and Hardraw. After half a kilometre, the path zigzags down on to the shoulder of Great Shunner Fell. Run down the path along the centre of the ridge, marked by the occasional cairn. Ignore the various 4x4/quad bike paths. Continue past a small tarn on the R. Shortly after, run past a cairn and descend to the point where the path kinks L at another stone cairn (SD 842 945) at **Black Hill Moss** 7.9km.

⑤ Bear L at the cairn and run up the path, over a small hill before running down the paved/rocky path again, to meet a bridleway 10.9km.

⑥ Turn L, signposted 'Hardraw', following the bridleway to a gate after 100 metres. Run downhill to a second path and track junction. Continue ahead through the gate and follow the walled track to the finish at **Hardraw** 13km.

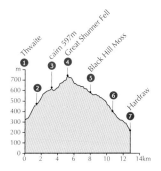

Route 27
Tan Hill (from Keld)

Start/finish	Park Lodge car park, Keld: NY 893 012
Distance	17.5km (10¾ miles)
Ascent	540m (1770ft)
Grade	Level 4
Time	2.5hr
Terrain	A mix of grassy tracks and smaller grassy paths across open moorland. Generally damp underfoot
Map	OS Landranger 91: Appleby-in-Westmorland
Refreshments	The Tan Hill Inn; Keld Lodge and Hotel; café in Muker
Public transport	Bus 30 from Richmond

This is a run with a truly remote and wild feel about it. For all that it follows the Pennine Way, it is rare to meet any one on this route. It is best run when the ground has had chance to dry out, due to the exposed nature of much of the route. The middle section could present some navigational difficulty in poor visibility.

The run begins by heading north from the ancient Norse hamlet of Keld and follows the clearly waymarked Pennine Way to the Tan Hill Inn, England's highest pub. This section contains most of the ascent, which is generally on good paths and tracks. The next section crosses an area of remote high moorland on small paths in a largely unfrequented part of the northern Dales, before dropping down to the tiny hamlet of Ravenseat. The final section runs alongside a small tributary of the River Swale and then follows the river itself downstream back to Keld.

Running along the Pennine Way towards the Tan Hill Inn

1. Leave the car park and follow the track, signposted 'Pennine Way', down towards the River Swale. Turn L at the track junction and descend the steep steps to the river. Run across the bridge and up the bank. The path then zig-zags up to the track close to the waterfall. Turn L, signposted 'Pennine Way', and run up the track to **East Stonesdale** 0.7km.

2. Pass through the gate and continue to climb steeply up a grassy walled lane that follows the Pennine Way up out of Swaledale. After a few hundred metres, continue ahead through a gate and out on to the open fell. The track flattens as it crosses through a second gate. Cross the rough pasture, heading for three stone barns. Run up the track, crossing a small stream, to a wall below **Frith Lodge** 2.6km.

3. Pass through the gate and run along the grassy track, past the barns, through several fields. Follow the Pennine Way across rough pasture to a small stream crossed by a stone footbridge and guarded by a solitary gate 4.2km.

4. A short muddy uphill section climbs on to **Stonesdale Moor**. Bear L on a small path, marked by a cairn. The path widens to become a track. Follow

 159

this to a second cairn and signpost. Bear R and ascend through old mine workings. Continue to run along the track, turning L at the signpost to the **Tan Hill Inn** 7km.

Featured and famous

Both the Tan Hill Inn and Ravenseat have featured in television shows. The Tan Hill Inn appeared in a 1980s double-glazing advert and Ravenseat appeared in *The Dales*, a series depicting life in the Yorkshire Dales.

---

5 Turn L along the road to a T junction. Turn L down the minor road for a couple of hundred metres to a footpath, signposted 'Ravenseat', and a stone marker. Turn R and descend SW over rough pasture to a small stream. Follow the path alongside the stream to the junction with a larger stream and a marker post. Turn L and follow the L bank (looking downstream), muddy in places, to a small wooden hut and stone sheepfolds 8.8km.

6 Turn R across the stone footbridge and climb the L side of the stream gully to a signpost. Follow the path and run up and across **Robert's Seat**. In bad

The Tan Hill Inn, Britain's highest pub

weather, this section may be hard to navigate. Continue for approximately 2km to a fence (11.2km – NY 871 041). Run along the path as it bears R past a ruined stone building. Bear L past a wooden post and TV aerial and run down through the fields to a ford just above Ravenseat Farm 12.2km.

7 Do not cross the ford, but take a small path on the L, leading to the farm buildings. Go straight ahead, through the gate, following the footpath,

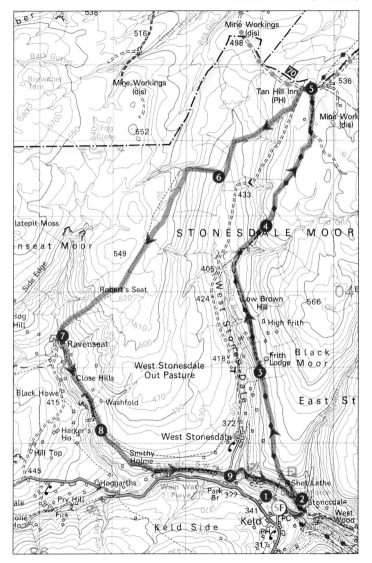

Sheep, a common sight on many of the runs

signposted 'Keld'. Follow this muddy path as it contours up past old stone barns high above the tributary of the River Swale. Follow the path to an indistinct path junction, just past an impressive gorge section of the river 13.2km.

8 Take the R path, signposted 'Keld', down to an old farmhouse. Turn L and run down the track towards the **River Swale**. Shortly before the river, bear L up and along a footpath next to a broken wall. Follow this path through several fields to a minor road 15.8km.

9 Cross the road and follow the stony bridleway down over the bridge above Currack Falls. Cross the river and climb the track back to waypoint 2, **East Stonesdale**. Follow the track back to the start 17.5km.

Route 28
Arkengarthdale

Start/finish	Roadside parking by minor road T junction to Whaw: NY 981 042
Distance	26.5km (16½ miles)
Ascent	540m (1770ft)
Grade	Level 5
Time	3hr 30min
Terrain	A mix of good stony tracks and small grassy tracks, some of which are faint or intermittent
Map	OS Landranger 92: Barnard Castle & Richmond; OS Explorer OL30: Yorkshire Dales Northern & Central Areas
Refreshments	CB Inn, Arkengarthdale; Tan Hill Inn; and plenty of shops and pubs in Reeth
Public transport	No nearby transport links

This is a remote, tough run with sections of small indistinct paths that require good levels of navigation and route-finding skills, especially in poor weather. The area is littered with the remains of old lead and coal mines, and care should be taken when approaching any of these areas.

The run follows a broad triangle around Arkengarthdale Moor. The first section starts on easy-to-follow broad tracks, which gradually become less and less distinct, finishing with 2km of indistinct paths to reach the Tan Hill Inn. The middle section is the easiest, following the Pennine Way across the high moorland to reach the remote Sleightholme Farm. The final section follows an intermittent path that crosses the watershed, back into Arkengarthdale.

Safety

Any small white plastic sticks along the route mark the location of the grit trays for the grouse and are not navigational aids. From West Moor to the Tan Hill Inn, the paths marked on the map are not always present on the ground. In poor weather consider using the 1:25,000 scale map (OL30: Yorkshire Dales Northern & Central Areas).

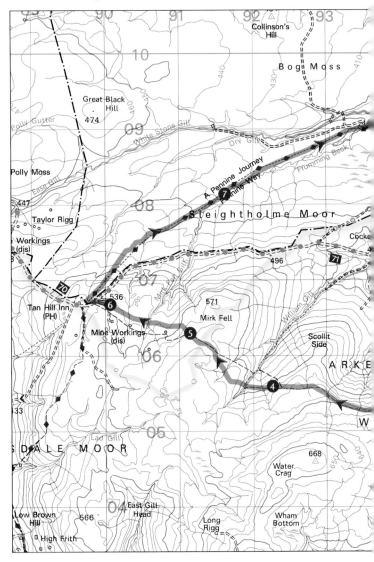

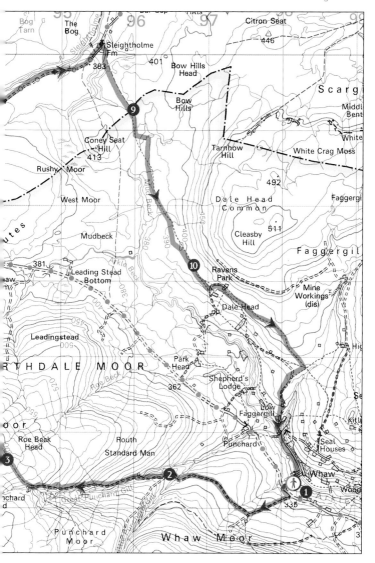

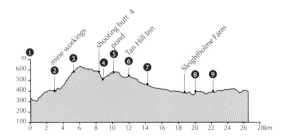

1 Run down the road towards Reeth for 100 metres. Turn R uphill along a stony track. Bear R at the track junction and run down the track over a stream and up the other side. Bear R at a second track junction and follow the track as it descends into the stream valley, crossing the stream at the mine workings 2.6km.

2 Run steeply up the track away from the mines. The track levels off after 100 metres before climbing again to the head of the valley and a track junction. Bear R, climbing past a fenced-off mine shaft, on to the moorland plateau of **West Moor**. After a few hundred metres, the track becomes a less distinct path through the heather, marked by the occasional white-topped post or cairn. Continue along to a small stream 5.4km.

3 Run along the small path, contouring above a steep slope around the head of a small river valley. Gradually descend before crossing a small spur, past a metal-capped mine shaft on the R. Follow the path through a line of shooting butts to reach a track at butt 4. Leave the track and run straight ahead, descending a small boggy path to a stream. Cross the stream to a track and small cairn at NY 918 055 8.6km.

4 Climb steeply up the bank on a faint path, not marked on the 1:50,000 map. Follow the path up across the moor to a stream junction. Bear R for

Shooting butt 'Number 4'

50 metres along the bank to a small cairn (partially hidden), next to a shooting butt. Cross the stream and bear R (330° magnetic) on a faint path to reach a cairn at NY 915 060. The cairn marks the point where the path on the ground rejoins the right of way on the 1:50,000 map. Run along the small path, marked occasionally with cairns, to a metal-capped mine shaft and small boundary stone. Bear L downhill, again following the path on the ground – not the right of way – to a small pond with a ruined building beyond 10.3km.

5 Bear R and follow the tiny path across the moor. After 200 metres descend across and over a steep-sided stream gully. Continue, heading W on the faint path before climbing a heather bank. After 400 metres, the path joins a grassy track close to a fenced-off mine shaft. Bear L and follow the track to meet a stony track. Turn R and follow this to the road and the **Tan Hill Inn** 11.7km.

6 Turn R before the inn and run down the Pennine Way. The route is marked by white-topped posts. The first section is boggy in places. Continue for a couple of kilometres to pass a circular stone sheep fold. Run ahead, dropping down to a stream and a large stone beehive-shaped cairn 14.1km.

7 Run along the stream on a good grassy path to reach a large green bridge. Cross the river and run along the track, still following the Pennine Way to a track junction 17.2km.

8 Turn L and run down the track to **Sleightholme Farm**. Turn R through the solid wooden gates and across the farmyard into the field. Descend through the field, bearing R through the second field to twin gates. Turn L up the track to the top of the steep bank and cross the field diagonally to a gate. Continue ahead for a short distance to reach a second gate 20km.

Stream cutting through the bedrock

9 Continue ahead, running on a small intermittent path through the tussock grass, parallel to a line of small ponds. When the path peters out, head for a large patch of rushes. Cross these (with a circular sheep fold on your L) and pick up a quad bike track. With the sheepfold directly behind you, follow the quad bike track across the moorland to reach a wall crossing and a rusty old farm trailer 22.3km.

10 Run ahead, following the track through the fields. Bear L up the track to Ravens Park Farm. Follow the grassy track in front of the farmhouse and through the field to a gate. Cross through the gate and back out on to the rough pasture. Turn R and follow the grassy quad bike track to a fence crossing. Continue ahead to a path junction. Run downhill, bear L at the fork and run down to the stream. Turn R along the path to meet a stony track. Bear R down the stony track, through a farm, to the road. Turn R and follow the road back to the start 26.5km.

Route 29
Pendragon Castle to Skipton Castle
Ultra Leg 2 (Hawes to Kettlewell)

Start	Hawes Youth Hostel: SD 867 897
Finish	Kettlewell Youth Hostel: SD 969 723
Distance	33km (20 miles)
Ascent	1115m (3660ft)
Grade	Level 2
Time	4hr 30min
Terrain	Mainly good grassy tracks and paths with short sections of stony tracks and road
Map	OS Landranger 98: Wensleydale & Upper Wharfedale
Refreshments	Hawes and Kettlewell have a range of shops, cafés and pubs
Public transport	Bus 830 from Ingleton; 856 from Leyburn; 875 from Grassington; S3 from Sedbergh

This is a straightforward scenic run that, in the main, follows the Pennine Way and Dales Way. Both these routes are well signposted and the navigation is straightforward. The run links the two major dales of Wensleydale and Wharfedale, crossing some remote and wild scenery. The first section includes most of the ascent, as it climbs out of Hawes following the Pennine Way. The summit of Dodd Fell is bypassed to the west before descending to Cam Houses. The middle section picks up the Dales Way and follows Oughtershaw Beck to its junction with Green Field Beck, forming the River Wharfe at Beckermonds. The run turns south-east, following riverside paths towards Buckden. The final section continues to follow the growing River Wharfe, as it flows through a wide valley to reach the village of Kettlewell.

On a high, and heading south

The run follows one of the most scenic sections of the Dales Way, a route that links Ilkley in the south to Bowness-on-Windermere in the north. The run joins the Dales Way at Cam Houses, its highest point, and follows the course of the River Wharfe as it flows south.

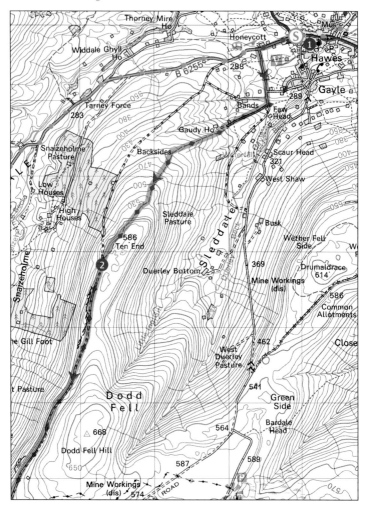

1 From the youth hostel turn L and run up the road (B6225) for 400 metres. Turn L, opposite a caravan park, following a small road until it meets the Pennine Way. Turn R up a farm track to a stone barn. Turn L, signposted

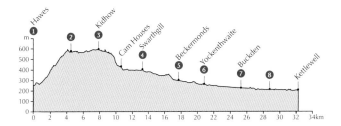

'Pennine Way', and climb steeply through the rough, muddy pasture, passing through the occasional gate. Continue to climb to reach a flat grassy section. Bear R and climb up over a shoulder to reach a gate. Run across the rough moorland for a few hundred metres, before descending to meet a stony track 4.6km.

2 Turn L, signposted 'Pennine Way', and run up the track leading towards **Dodd Fell**. Continue to follow the track as it contours around the mountain. After a few kilometres, the track levels out and, soon after, reaches the minor road at **Kidhow** 8.4km.

3 Turn R and run along the road, passing over a cattle grid, to a track and road junction. Turn L and descend the track towards Camm Farm. Bear L at the track junction and descend to **Cam Houses**. Turn L at the farm and follow the Dales Way signs through the buildings and run down through the fields on a grassy path to a ruined, roofless barn. Turn L over a small stream and run along the Dales Way through several fields, over streams and through small patches of regenerated woodland to reach the farm at **Swarthgill** 12.9km.

Runner competing in the '3 Peaks Ultra'

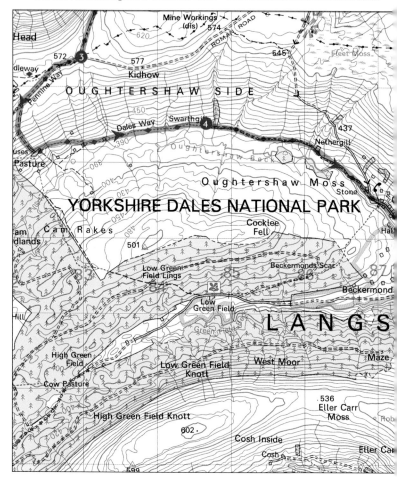

4 Take the track to the R of the farm, cross the stream and run down a rough tarmac track past Nethergill Farm to join the minor road at the hamlet of **Oughtershaw**. Turn R and run along the road, through Oughtershaw, before dropping steeply down to a road junction at the top of Wharfedale 17km.

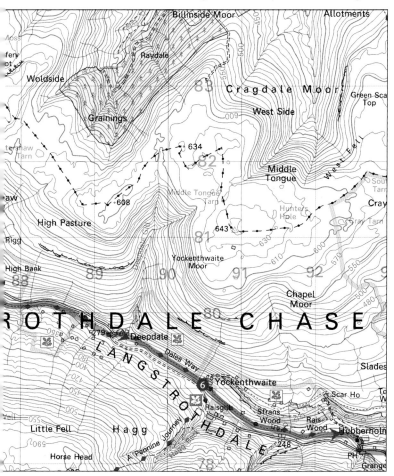

5 Turn R down the 'No Through Road' to **Beckermonds**. Turn L just after cross-ing the river and take the track to a second river. Cross the foot bridge and turn L downstream to a path junction. Bear L, signposted 'Dales Way'. Run down the rocky path alongside the river. The path soon becomes grassy, before changing to a stony track, as it gradually descends to meet the road at

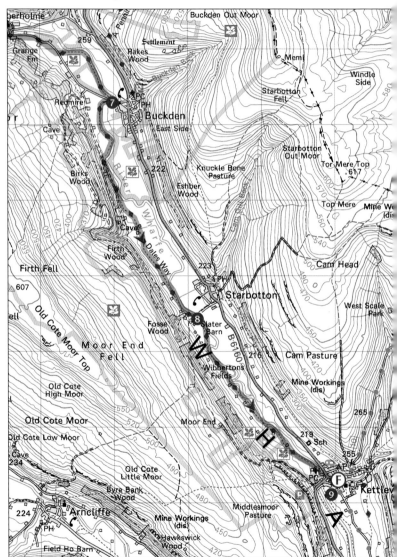

Deepdale. Turn L over the bridge and immediately R along the farm track. Turn R before the farm and follow the grassy footpath, signposted 'Yockenthwaite', down through the field to a small footbridge. Bear L around the edge of the field to a gate. Go through the gate and descend to the **River Wharfe**. Run along the grassy riverside track to Yockenthwaite Farm 20.9km.

6 Bear R, in front of the farm, descending across the grass to a track. Turn L along the track through the gate. Bear R down to the river. Run along the grassy paths and tracks to the church at **Hubberholme**. Follow the track past the church, crossing the road to the George Inn. Turn L and run along the road for approximately 800 metres. Turn L through the field and run along the riverside path to rejoin the road at **Buckden** 25.5km.

7 Cross the road, bearing R along the river, signposted the 'Dales Way'. Run through the fields next to the river before bearing R up to a gate. Follow the path up to a track. Turn L and run down the track, passing a large stone barn for a few hundred metres. Turn L, signposted 'Dales Way', following the track through the fields, crossing a small stream to a walled lane. Continue to follow the grassy track around the edge of the fields back to the river. Run ahead to the footbridge and fingerpost at **Starbotton** 29km.

8 Continue ahead, signposted 'Kettlewell', alongside the river. Shortly after, the path leaves the riverside, before rejoining it again; this pattern is repeated for the next few kilometres. The path eventually leads to a walled lane and the riverside path that leads to the road bridge at **Kettlewell**. Turn L across the river, following the road into the village. Cross a second smaller river and turn R up to the hostel 33km.

The upper River Wharfe just east of Beckermonds

SOUTH-EAST DALES AND WHARFEDALE

Crossing the stream at the top of Troller's Gill (photo: Adrian Dellbridge) (Route 35)

Route 30
Bolton Abbey

Start/finish	Bolton Abbey car park: SE 071 539
Distance	12km (7½ miles)
Ascent	220m (720ft)
Grade	Level 2
Time	1hr 30min
Terrain	Good paths and tracks all the way
Map	OS Landranger 98: Wensleydale & Upper Wharfedale
Refreshments	The Cavendish Pavilion serves food all year round
Public transport	Buses 874 and 875 from Ilkley/Skipton; bus 74 from Ilkley/ Grassington

This is a straightforward run that takes in the best parts of the popular Bolton Abbey Estate. The run visits both the ruins of Bolton Abbey and The Strid, combined with an undulating run through the wooded valley of the River Wharfe. Bolton Abbey was a 12th-century Augustinian monastery before it was destroyed in the Dissolution of the Monasteries. The nave survives and is used as a parish church today. The Strid is a narrow section of rock that forces the River Wharfe through a six-foot wide gorge. The rocks on either side are heavily undercut, causing strong currents and undertows that give The Strid its fearsome reputation.

The run starts through the ruined abbey, before following the popular riverside tourist path to The Strid. The route continues to follow the River Wharfe upstream, before crossing to the other bank and following good paths through scenic woodland back to the start.

① Leave the car park and run past the village shop and information centre. Turn R along the road to the T junction. Cross the road and pass through the stone arch, signposted Priory Church. Run down the steps to the ruined **Bolton Abbey**. Follow the path around in front of the abbey to the road. Run along the footpath to the Cavendish monument. Turn R at the monument. Take a small path down the steep steps and across the fields to a large car park.

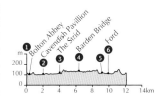

Bear L and follow the river a short distance to the **Cavendish Pavilion** café and toilets 1.9km.

Priory Church

Bolton Abbey's Priory Church is one of the Yorkshire Dale's most visited locations, attracting over 160,000 people a year.

---

2 Run past the café, following the L bank of the river, through a gate, signposted 'The Strid'. Follow the main track for approximately 500 metres to a track junction. Take the R fork downhill to the riverside. Bear L along the track and run up past the Wood Bodger's camp. Continue along the track to reach **The Strid** 4km.

3 Bear L up a small rocky path that rises above The Strid before levelling off. Take the L fork at the first path junction and R at the next fork, signposted 'Barden Bridge'. Run along the riverside path to a stone bridge. Follow the path under the bridge to the road junction at **Barden Bridge** 6.2km.

The narrow, rocky section of the River Wharfe known as The Strid

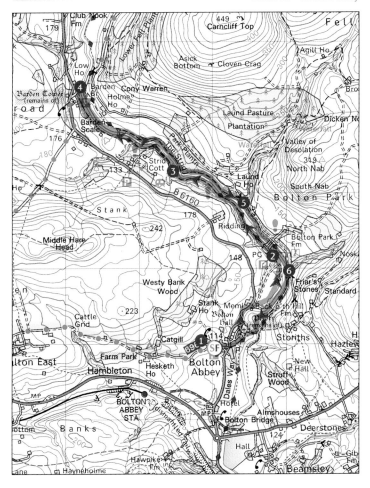

④ Turn R over the bridge and immediately R through the grassy fields as you now head back down stream. Run down the path, past the stone bridge and up into the woodland. Follow the high-level path back down to overlook The Strid, before continuing to a small wooden shelter. Continue ahead down to a small wooden bridge over a stream 9.2km.

Bridge over the River Wharfe at the Cavendish Pavilion

⑤ Cross the bridge, signposted 'Cavendish Pavilion' and 'Bolton Abbey'. Run along the path as it first follows the riverside, before rising up and over the wooden bridge to the Cavendish Pavilion. Do not cross the bridge. Instead take the small footpath on the opposite river bank. Run along the path to meet a road. Turn L and cross the stream via a ford. Follow the road for 50 metres to a footpath 10.3km.

⑥ Turn R along the footpath to a fork. Take the L fork and climb steeply up and away from the river. Continue ahead at the next junction, heading back towards the abbey ruins, before bearing L down to the stepping stones and wooden bridge over the river. Cross the bridge and follow the path back to the stone arch and back to the start 12km.

Route 31
Simon's Seat

Start/finish	Roadside car park, Barden Bridge: SE 052 574
Distance	13.5km (8.4 miles)
Ascent	460m (1510ft)
Grade	Level 2
Time	2hr
Terrain	A mixture of good stony paths and tracks with a small section of boggy path around the summit of Simon's Seat
Map	OS Landranger 98: Wensleydale & Upper Wharfedale
Refreshments	Café at Barden Tower; pubs and shops at Burnsall; Cavendish Pavilion café at Bolton Abbey
Public transport	Bus 874 to Strid Wood from Ilkley/Skipton

This is a popular, beautiful run that follows one of the Dale's best known rivers, the Wharfe, before climbing up through the Valley of Desolation to the high point of Simon's Seat. The first section runs downstream from the start, following a good path through the wooded valley of the River Wharfe, past a narrow rapid known as The Strid. The second section climbs up through a wooded valley and pine forest on to the open moor. A steep ascent leads to the summit plateau, crossing it to reach the gritstone outcrop of Simon's Seat. The final section descends across the moor, through a second pine forest, to reach the River Wharfe higher upstream, which is followed back down to the start. The run is best completed in either spring when the moorland birds are calling or in late summer when the purple heather is in full bloom. The run crosses access land of the Bolton Abbey Estate (Barden Moor/Fell). Restrictions may be in place during the shooting season. Dogs are not permitted, as part of the agreement.

1 From the car park, follow the riverside path, through the field, downstream with the **River Wharfe** on your R. After a short distance, this becomes a stony path. Continue to run downstream to a large stone aqueduct/bridge Continue on the L bank, as the path rises to a gate 1.1km.

2 Pass through the gate and run through the woodland on a good path that undulates above the river. In places, the path is narrow and there are steep drops to the R. After a few hundred metres, the river rapid known as **The Strid** can be seen below. Follow the path past a small stone shelter, before dropping down to run alongside the river. Eventually, the path reaches a small road and wooden bridge across a stream 3km.

3 Leave the path and take the road, signposted 'Valley of Desolation', uphill for 100 metres. Turn L, past an information board, and follow the track up through the fields to a gate. Continue ahead on the grassy track, which is

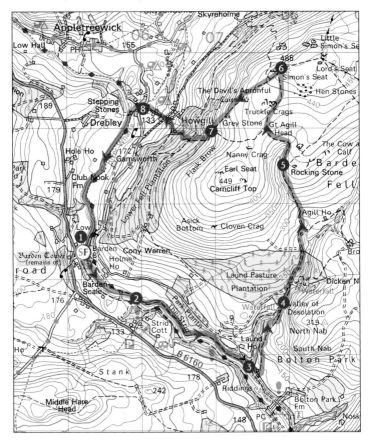

muddy in places, past a pond on the R, to the steep wooded valley and waterfall. (There is a small path that leads you to the waterfall if you want a closer view.) The run continues up and around to meet a path coming in from the R. Turn L on to it and run uphill between two wire fences. The path narrows and then descends into the **Valley of Desolation** and a footbridge 4.4km.

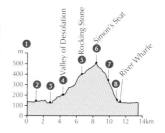

The Valley of Desolation

The Valley of Desolation took on its name after a storm in the early 1800s washed away large parts of the valley.

4 Cross the footbridge and run up the small path alongside the stream for 100 metres, before it climbs steeply up, away from the stream, to a gate. Pass through the gate and run up the steep stony track through the pine forest, signposted 'Simon's Seat'. After a few hundred metres, the track levels off and the edge of the forest is reached. Run along the track out on to the open moor. After 300metres, the track descends, crosses a small stream and then ascends steeply up **Barden Fell**. Follow this to a track junction close to the **Rocking Stone** 6.6km.

Running through Strid Wood (photo: Adrian Dellbridge)

5 Run up the track as it turns L across the moor and rises to

the summit plateau, to reach a track fork. Take the R fork on to a muddy/rocky path that leads past large gritstone boulders, up to the rocky summit of **Simon's Seat**. Just before the summit, a small path branches off to the L; this is the return path. Climb the summit rocks to the trig point at 485m 8.3km.

Following the River Wharfe downstream (photo: Adrian Dellbridge)

6 Climb back down from the summit and take the small path (to the L if facing the trig point), which is paved in places, to a small section of wooden fence at the base of a rocky outcrop. Run down the small path, now gravel, as it drops towards the Wharfe valley. The way is marked by the occasional stone cairn and the path becomes rockier and muddier. Continue down to meet a stone wall. Bear L along the wall to meet a track 9.8km.

7 Run down the track, signposted 'Howgill', zigzagging through the forest to a gate. Continue to follow the track down to a second gate and minor road crossing. Go straight across and take the small track down past the houses to a road 11.3km.

8 Cross the road and follow the track, signposted 'Dales Way/Barden Bridge', through the farm buildings and a small collection of caravans, to reach the **River Wharfe**. Turn L and run along the riverside path through the fields back to the start 13.5km.

Route 32
Malham Cove and Gordale Scar

Start/finish	Malham National Park Visitor Centre: SD 900 627
Distance	11.5km (7 miles)
Ascent	220m (720ft)
Grade	Level 3
Time	1hr 30min
Terrain	Mainly hard tracks, stone paths and grassy paths with a very short section of road. The scramble up Gordale Scar and the limestone pavement and steps of Malham Cove are slippy, especially when wet
Map	OS Landranger 98: Wensleydale & Upper Wharfedale
Refreshments	Pubs, cafés and shops in Malham
Public transport	Buses 75, 210, 211, 873 and 884 from Skipton

This is a short circular route that encompasses two of the Yorkshire Dale's finest geological features. The run starts at the National Park Centre in Malham and follows a scenic route to the waterfall of Janet's Foss. The route then crosses into the stunning limestone gorge of Gordale Scar, exiting via a short scramble alongside the waterfall into a dry valley. Easy grassy running brings you to Malham Tarn – a relic of the Ice Age – before returning to the start, via one of the country's finest limestone features: Malham Cove, an impressive 300-foot high limestone cliff.

Safety

To avoid the scramble up Gordale Scar, after joining the road from Janet's Foss, take the footpath on the left (signposted 'Malham Cove'). Follow the road for approximately 300 metres, turn right and follow a small grassy path that leads up and over New Close Knotts to rejoin the path leading from Gordale Scar.

---

① From the car park turn L. Run along the road for 100 metres. Turn R immediately before the Malham Smithy and cross the river via a stone slab bridge. Run along the footpath, signposted 'Janet's Foss' and 'Gordale'. Turn L at the first kissing gate and follow the path through the fields to enter a small wooded limestone gorge. Continue to **Janet's Foss** 1.9km.

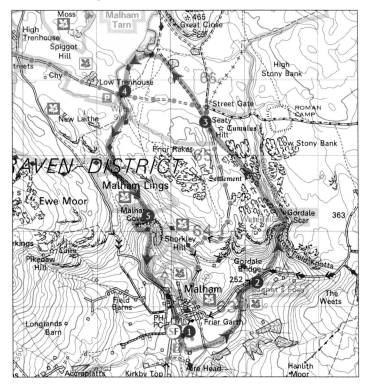

A queen's force

Janet's Foss is so named because it is the waterfall (force) of Janet, queen of the local fairies. The foss, a 15-foot waterfall, is formed as Gordale Beck flows over a band of limestone, which is more resistant to erosion by water.

2 Follow the path to the road. Turn R for 100 metres to a small campsite. Turn L, signposted 'Gordale Scar', and follow the path into the impressive limestone gorge. The route exits **Gordale Scar** by a short easy scramble, with good handholds up alongside the waterfall. CARE does need to be taken as the rock can be slippy and wet. Use common sense and knowledge of your own ability. Start at the foot of the water-fall and climb a few feet into a big scoop. Ignore what looks to be an easier route straight upwards out of the scoop. Step L for a few feet and up to the top, using good footholds and handholds, into the impressive natural amphitheatre of limestone arches and falls behind. Follow the small path up the L side that leads steeply up and out of the gorge. The path now becomes flat and grassy. Run through small patches of limestone pavement to meet the road, just before **Street Gate** 4.3km.

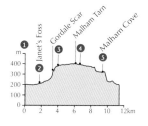

3 Turn R along the road to the track junction (as the road bends L). Run ahead along the track towards **Malham Tarn**. After approximately half a kilometre, turn L, following a grassy path past a small wood to the tarn. Turn L, following the small path to the National Trust car park 6.3km.

4 From the car park, turn R. Run along the road for 50 metres, then turn L following the Pennine Way. At the path junction, take the L fork running along the grassy path to a wall (do not cross). Bear R, signposted 'Dry Valley', along a rocky path into a small limestone valley. Run along the path to a stile at the head of a dry valley. Turn sharp L and descend the rocky path to **Malham Cove** 9.1km.

The impressive natural amphitheatre of Malham Cove

Halfway up the scramble out of Gordale Scar

5 Turn R across the limestone pavement, signposted 'Pennine Way'. Take CARE not to get too close to the edge. Cross to the R end of the cove. Descend via the steep steps to the bottom of the cove. Turn R and follow the path back to the road. Turn R back to **Malham** 11.5km.

Route 33
Mastiles Lane

Start/finish	Malham Tarn car park at Low Trenhouse: SD 894 658
Distance	25.5km (16 miles)
Ascent	640m (2100ft)
Grade	Level 1
Time	3hr 30min
Terrain	A mix of good stony and grassy tracks and bridleways; occasionally boggy in places
Map	OS Landranger 98: Wensleydale & Upper Wharfedale
Refreshments	Cafés and pubs in Malham
Public transport	Malham is the closest village; multiple buses from Skipton

This is a fantastic trail run following one of the Yorkshire Dale's best known tracks. Mastiles Lane is an ancient track that links Malhamdale with Wharfedale at Kilnsey, famous for its overhanging limestone crag and for having one of the oldest fell races in England.

The route follows a broad triangle. The first section follows Mastiles Lane eastwards, before dropping down to Winterburn Reservoir on a series of excellent tracks, leaving behind the classic limestone scenery for that of millstone grit. The middle section typifies the saying 'for every down there is an up'; the route climbs steadily up on a series of tracks and walled lanes back into limestone country, before a superb descent to the eastern end of Mastiles Lane. The final section of the route follows the track up and westwards as it crosses Kilnsey Moor. It is worth saving a bit in your legs for this last section as it begins with a kilometre-long stiff climb.

> ### Safety
>
> While there are no mountain ascents, this is a high-level route that can be exposed to the weather.

1 Turn L out of the car park and run along the road for a few hundred metres before the road turns sharp R. Here, continue straight ahead to **Street Gate**. Pass through the gate and continue ahead on the Mastiles Lane track, sign-posted 'Kilnsey'. Run down the track and over a small stream, before climbing up to a large stone containing information on the **Roman Marching Camp**. Continue ahead, following the track as it becomes a walled lane. Run along the lane to a track bridleway junction 3.8km.

 189

2 Turn R along the bridleway, signposted 'Lea Gate'. Follow the track through the fields as it bears L, then R, becoming a walled lane to meet a road. Continue ahead on the road. As the road begins drop towards Malham, Turn L on a bridleway, signposted 'Weets Top'. Run up the steep track to a gate marked by an old market stone. Pass through the gate 6.6km.

3 Run down the L hand track, signposted 'Hetton', across rough pasture to a wall. Cross through the wall and bear R on the grassy path, then bear L around the small grassy hill. Follow the track as it twists and turns downhill through several gates for a couple of kilometres towards **Winterburn Reservoir**. Continue down to cross the head of the reservoir on a stone bridge 9.8km.

4 Turn L over the bridge and run up the track, as it zigzags above the reservoir, to meet Moor Lane: a junction of tracks and bridleways. Do not pass through the gate, but turn sharp L, following a grassy track, signposted 'Boss Moor', as it climbs up to a gate. Continue through the gate and run along the walled track to a road 11.7km.

5 Turn L along the road. Take the first bridleway on the R, signposted 'Moor Lane' and 'Threshfield'. After a few metres, take the L fork (ahead), following the grassy track gently upwards to a wall corner (SD 958 630). Turn L through the gate, signposted 'Malham Moor Lane'. Continue ahead through the gate and follow the walled lane to its end. Bear L along the track as it descends to a

Kilnsey Crag with Mastiles Lane (top left of the picture)

double gate and the ruined **Height Laithe Farm**. Run past the farm, following the blue marker posts up to the road that crosses **Malham Moor** 15.5km.

(6) Cross the road, signposted 'Kilnsey', and follow the blue marker posts across the fields and up on to the open fell. Run ahead to a gate marked with two large wooden posts. Pass through the gate and run down the grassy track towards **Mastiles Lane**. Just before rejoining the lane, take the R fork down to the wall. Follow this through the sheep pens to Mastiles Lane 17.8km.

Mastiles Lane climbing up and over Kilnsey Moor

Mastiles Lane

Mastiles Lane is as an ancient drove track, originally used by the Romans but also by the great northern abbeys to move wool and other goods from their grange at Kilnsey to Malham. Modern day farmers use it for much the same reason, and it is a very popular walking and mountain biking route.

(7) Turn L and begin a steady climb up Mastiles lane to reach a high point of 428m. Run along the track before descending to a gate. Continue ahead through the gate and run along the track towards the **Roman Camp** and Street Gate. After a couple of kilometres, the run rejoins the outward leg of the route. Retrace the route back to the start 25.5km.

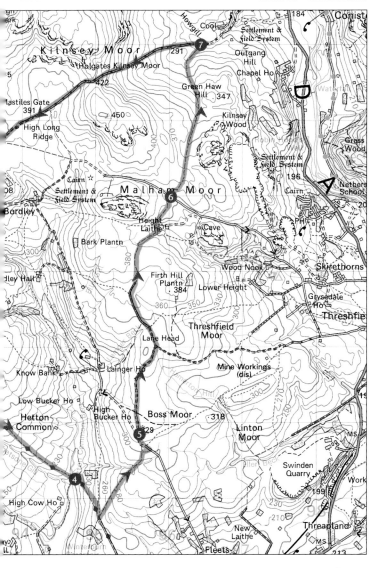

Route 34
Grass Wood and Conistone Dib

Start/finish	YDNP Visitor Centre: SE 002 636
Distance	13km (8 miles)
Ascent	320m (1050ft)
Grade	Level 1
Time	2hr
Terrain	A mixture of excellent, mainly grassy, paths, with short sections of track and road
Map	OS Landranger 98: Wensleydale & Upper Wharfedale
Refreshments	Grassington has a wide range of shops, cafés and pubs
Public transport	Multiple buses to Grassington

This is an absolutely superb run, best completed on a spring evening, when the woodland flowers are in bloom and the curlews and other waders are calling. It is one of the best short runs in the Dales. The first section quickly leaves Grassington and passes through Grass Wood, followed by a short section of road leading to Conistone. The next section passes through the fantastic Conistone Dib and meets the Dales Way. The final section follows the Dales Way through the fields back to Grassington.

1 Turn L out of the car park and follow the road to Grassington. Turn R after 100 metres, into the village centre and run up Main Street. Turn L in front of the Devonshire Institute and follow the road to Town Head. Bear L downhill in front of Dales Dairies, to a road and track junction. Turn R along the track and follow the walled lane towards Grass Wood, to reach a sharp L bend and fingerpost 1.7km.

2 Run along the track, past a stone barn, to twin gates. Take the gate on the R. At the end of the first field, bear R to the entrance of **Grass Wood**. Run up the small footpath, passing the information board, as you climb up into the wood. Follow the well-made path up and through the wooded limestone valley to a path crossroads, marked by a signpost. Continue ahead, signposted 'Grass Wood Lane'. After 50 metres, turn R, signposted 'footpath'. Run along the small path through the woods, following the occasional yellow marker posts. After a few hundred metres, the path turns sharply L. Run downhill to meet a track. Run down the track to the road 4.4km.

3 Turn R along the road and then R again, taking a small footpath through the field to rejoin the road. Run N along the road, for approximately 1.5 km, to a T junction in the hamlet of **Conistone** 6.3km.

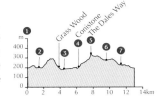

4 Turn R and immediately R along a track to meet the gate and fingerpost at the entrance to **Conistone Dib**. Ascend the rock steps and take the rocky path into the limestone gorge. Run up the dry rocky bed of the old stream, between the sheer walls of the gorge, passing through a narrow rock slot into the valley behind. Run along the path, between the scree slopes, uphill to the gate. Continue to run up the valley. Take the L fork at the footpath junction to a second gate. Follow the path alongside the wall, as it enters a second gorge section. Climb steeply up through a small gate, to scramble up through the limestone escarpment and meet the **Dales Way** path 7.9km.

Conistone Dib

Conistone Dib is an atmospheric rocky limestone gorge entered through a narrow passage.

---

5 Turn R along the broad grassy path back towards Grassington. Run along the path to a wall and footpath junction. Take the R fork, signposted 'Dales Way footpath'. Run along the path, over several walls and down past an old lime kiln on the R, to a wall junction 9.5km.

6 Run along the path next to the fence, to a footpath junction. Take the L fork and run uphill through small patches of limestone pavement. After

The narrowest section of Conistone Dib

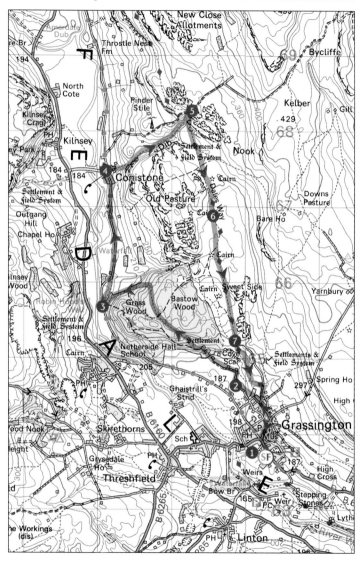

Ash trees and limestone pavement, common features of this part of the Dales

approximately 1km, the path becomes a track. Continue to run along the track as it drops towards Grassington. At the track junction, take the R fork and R again at a second junction, to reach a wall, signposted 'Dales Way footpath' 11.2km.

 Cross the wall and run a short distance to a second wall. Pass through the stile and turn L, following the grassy path through the fields, heading towards a farm (the other side of Dales Dairies from the outbound route). Just before the farm, turn L along the footpath through the fields to meet a track. Turn R along the track and follow it to the end. Turn L and follow the road, retracing the outward route back down into **Grassington** to the start 13km.

Route 35
Troller's Gill

Start/finish	Grimwith Reservoir car park and toilets: SE 063 639
Distance	17km (10½ miles)
Ascent	385m (1260ft)
Grade	Level 3
Time	2hr 30min
Terrain	Mainly on good tracks and small grassy paths with short sections of road. The short section through Troller's Gill follows the course of a rocky stream bed
Map	OS Landranger 98: Wensleydale & Upper Wharfedale; OS Landranger 99: Northallerton & Ripon
Refreshments	Pub in the small village of Hebden; Grassington has a wide range of shops.
Public transport	Bus 825 from Grassington/Ripon

This is a good trail run, especially in late summer or early autumn when the heather is in full bloom. The route starts with a gentle circuit of Grimwith Reservoir, one of the largest bodies of water in Yorkshire, before crossing to Stump Cross Caverns, one of the Yorkshire Dale's limestone show caves. The second section follows good tracks, finishing with a long descent to Skyreholme and Parceval Hall and Gardens. The next section passes through the picturesque limestone gorge of Troller's Gill, named after the mythical trolls that used to inhabit the gorge. A final short section of green lanes and tracks leads back to the start.

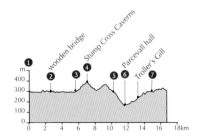

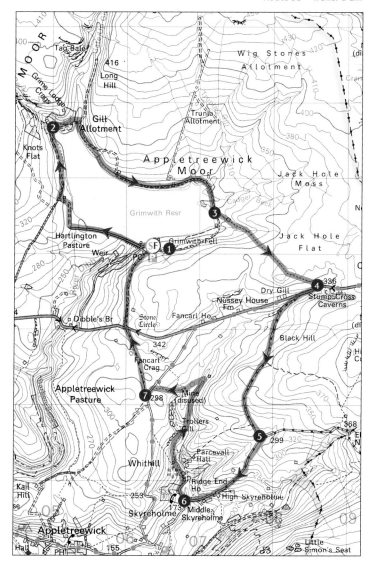

1. From the car park, run down the road to the reservoir embankment. Turn R through the gate and L along the embankment to a gate. Turn R and follow the walled track, with the **reservoir** on the R. Bear L uphill, past a stone barn, to a track junction. Turn R, sign-posted 'reservoir footpath', and run down the track to the wooden bridge 2.7km.

Running south down the track to Skyreholme (photo: Adrian Dellbridge)

2. Cross the bridge and run around the reservoir to cross another stream to a track junction. Bear R and follow the track to a junction after a few hundred metres. Take the foot-path that contours alongside the reservoir. Rejoin the track, running past an old ruined farmhouse, to the eastern end of the reservoir. Follow the track over a small embankment and then uphill to a track and footpath junction 5.7km.

3. Leave the reservoir, signposted 'Stump Cross 1¼ miles', and run up a small grassy path across the fields, past a barn to a ladder stile. Cross the stile on to the open moorland. Continue to run uphill to a wall and stiles. Bear R and follow the yellow marker posts. The path is joined from the L by a quad bike track. Bear R to reach a broken wall. Follow the path L (the quad bike track goes R at a line of shake holes) to wall junction and two consecutive ladder stiles. Cross the stiles and run down the grassy path to the B6265 at **Stump Cross Caverns** 7.7km.

4. Turn R and run down the road. Take CARE; it is a fast road with no pavement. After 300 metres, turn L on to the track, signposted 'Skyreholme'. Run down the track to a junction. Take the L fork and follow the track up alongside a wall to the reach the highpoint of the run at 360m. Continue to run along the track, through a gate and then steeply down to a track junction 10.3km.

Running through Troller's Gill (photo: Adrian Dellbridge)

5 Bear R downhill and follow the track, which changes to a road, down to the hamlet of **Skyreholme**. Follow this to a T junction. Bear R, signposted 'No Through Road' and 'Parceval Hall', and follow the road to a footpath on the L, just before the river 12km.

Did you know?

The 24-acre garden at Parceval Hall is the only RHS-registered garden in the YDNP and is open to the public. The gardens contain many excellent examples of plants from the Himalayas and China.

---

6 Turn L on to the path and run alongside the river, passing through a gate into the woodland at the entrance of **Troller's Gill**. Follow the path past a ruined barn to a gate and stile and through to a second gate. After a few metres, the public right of way footpath bears L uphill. Instead, bear R, taking the small permissive path heading to Troller's Gill. Run down the path to the stream and follow it to a stile. Cross the stile and follow the dry stream bed through a narrow limestone gorge (Troller's Gill). Take CARE if the limestone is wet: this section of route may be impassable after heavy rain. After approximately 300 metres, a second stile is reached. Cross this stile and run up alongside the stream to cross a third stile, and then cross the stream via a small wooden footbridge. Follow the steep footpath up through the newly planted woodland to rejoin the track and public right of way. Turn R and follow the track for 100 metres and then bear L at a sharp track bend. Run around the new plantation, following a small grassy path to the road. Turn L and follow the road for 50 metres to a road and track junction 14.8km.

7 Run up the grassy track, signposted 'B6265'. Follow the track to the road. Cross the road and take the track, signposted 'Grimwith Reservoir'. Run along the track back to the car park 17km.

Route 36
Great Whernside (from Kettlewell)

Start/finish	Kettlewell public car park and toilets: SD 968 723
Distance	12.5km (7¾ miles)
Ascent	595m (1950ft)
Grade	Level 3
Time	2hr
Terrain	A mixture of stone and grassy tracks, short boggy sections and steep grassy paths
Map	OS Landranger 98: Wensleydale & Upper Wharfedale
Refreshments	Shops, pubs and cafés in Kettlewell
Public transport	Bus 874/875 from Grassington/Hawes

Great Whernside dominates the village of Kettlewell, rising high above the village and the valley of the River Wharfe. The area is dotted with ancient lead mines dating from the Middle Ages and boasts some impressive dry-stone-wall scenery, built in the times of the Augustine monks.

This run forms a circuit of Park Gill Beck. Apart from the two steep climbs, the route is generally flat and runnable. The final descent back into Kettlewell is one of the best descents off any mountain in the Dales, and it is worth saving a bit in your legs for this last fast section.

The first section starts with a steep pull out of the valley, followed by good running to contour around to the road at Park Rash. The next section involves a second steep climb, up on to and along the broad summit ridge of Great Whernside. The final section takes a direct line back to the village, beginning at the summit and heading down to the Scout Association Hostel of Hag Dyke, before the fast, grassy descent back to Kettlewell.

1 Leave the public car park and turn L over the bridge. Turn R immediately and run along the road, with the river on the R. Continue ahead at the first road junction (shop on the right). The road steepens and bends L. After a couple of hundred metres, the road bends sharply R. Continue ahead at this point and run up the steep, stony track, signposted 'Starbotton' and 'Coverdale'. Continue to a gate at **Cam Pasture** 1.2km.

2 Run up the grassy walled track through a second and third gate, climbing high above the valley. Looking R, the whole of the route can be seen.

Continue to follow the grassy track, to reach a track junction marked by a fingerpost 3.5km.

3 Take the R fork, signposted 'Hunters Sleet'. Continue to a gate. Pass through the gate and run along a small rising path, which contours around the head of the valley. The path runs roughly parallel to a stone wall. After roughly 1km, pass through a double gate, taking time to view the ascent path up Great Whernside, which rises bottom L to a wall top R. At the path fork, take the R fork leading to the road 5.4km.

Great Whernside

Great Whernside is the middle of the three Whernside mountains in the Dales. It is higher than its near neighbour, Little Whernside, by some 100m and just lower than Yorkshire's highest mountain, Whernside, by 32m.

4 Cross the road and follow the grassy path, signposted 'Great Whernside', to the foot of the escarpment. At the path fork, take the R fork down a small dip and up to a gate. Pass through the gate, bearing R across a boggy section that climbs steeply up, heading for a stile in the wall and a fence just below the summit ridge. Cross the stile and continue up a rising traverse to

Running along the track above Wharfedale (photo: Adrian Dellbridge)

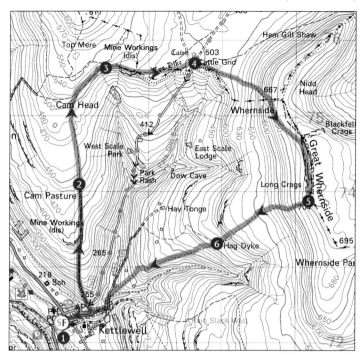

the summit ridge. Bear R and run on a grassy path across the boulder field. Follow the yellow-topped wooden marker posts to the summit trig point and the large stone cairn of **Great Whernside** 704m 8.2km.

5. Continue past the cairn for 20 metres and turn R, heading SW down a small path towards Kettlewell. Cross the first boggy section, still following the occasional yellow marker posts, to the top of a small rocky escarpment, marked by a stone cairn. Descend steeply down the escarpment to the old farmhouse of **Hag Dyke** 9.8km.

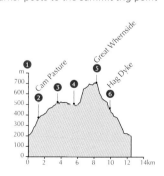

Finishing down Great Whernside as part of the FRA Relays (photo: Alex Pilkington)

6 Pass around the lower side of the farmhouse and through a small gate, marked 'Footpath'. Bear L through the field to the entrance gate, past the information board. Go through the gate and turn L, signposted 'Kettlewell'. Follow the grassy path across several fields and walls, marked by the occasional fingerpost, downhill towards the village. At the river, turn R along the bank for a few metres and L along a farm track to meet a tarmac road. Turn R along the road, which leads back into the centre of **Kettlewell** 12.5km.

Route 37
Fountains Fell

Start/finish	Roadside parking near Arncliffe: SD 930 719
Distance	25.5km (16 miles)
Ascent	630m (2070ft)
Grade	Level 2
Time	3hr 30min
Terrain	A mix of grassy paths and good tracks
Map	OS Landranger 98: Wensleydale & Upper Wharfedale
Refreshments	Falcon Inn, Arncliffe
Public transport	Buses 72 and 76 from Grassington to Kilnsey are the closest

This is one of the best runs in the book. The first section starts with a strenuous climb through classic limestone scenery, before descending to Malham Tarn, one of England's highest lakes. A short section around the tarn and through farmland is followed by a straightforward ascent and descent of Fountains Fell. The final section is a gentle run back down Littondale. Navigating this run is straightforward, with easy-to-follow paths and tracks, many of which are part of the Pennine Way.

> ### Safety
>
> If the River Skirfare is in flood, consider crossing the river at Litton and run back down the road to Arncliffe.

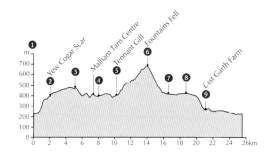

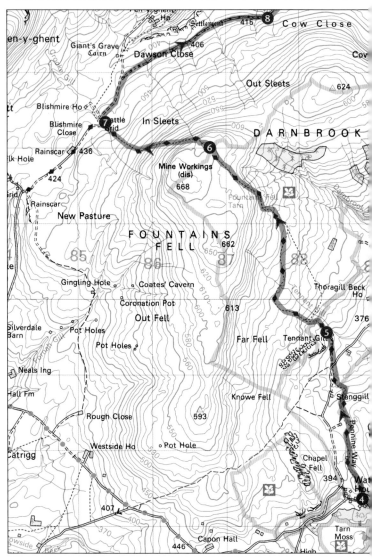

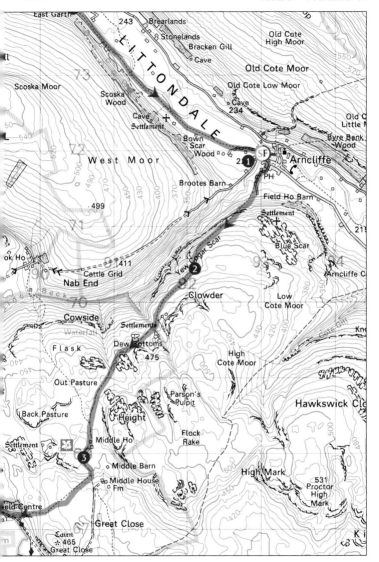

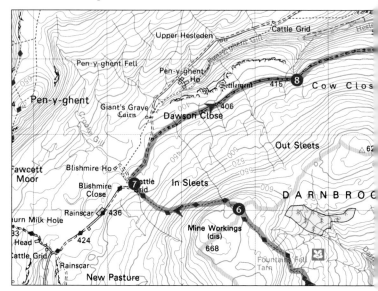

Stone cairns on the summit of Fountains Fell

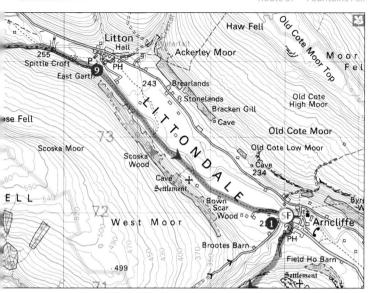

① Run over the bridge into Arncliffe. Turn R alongside the Falcon Inn and follow the track out towards the open fell. After a few hundred metres, the track begins to rise. Turn R on to the footpath, signposted 'Malham'. Climb steeply up through the field towards **Yew Cogar Scar**. Take the R path at the fork and continue to climb up on a small grassy path. After approximately 1km, the slope lessens. Run along the escarpment to reach a wall 2km.

② Continue to run along the footpath, over a small stream gully and past stone cairns. Eventually, the path bears L away from the main valley to reach a wall at the head of a steep stream gully. Cross the wall into Malham Tarn National Trust Estate and bear L through a shallow limestone valley on a good path to reach an abandoned farm 4.9km.

③ Take the rough track to the R of the farm, alongside the wall. Continue ahead as the wall turns L for 100 metres, then descend L to a gate. Pass through the gate and descend diagonally R, through the field to a stile. Cross the stile and run up and over a low col, before dropping down to the stony track at **Malham Tarn**. Turn R, signposted 'Pennine Way' and run along up through the woodland to **Malham Tarn Field Centre**. Pass around to the R and back of the centre and follow the track down to a junction at **Waterhouses** 7.8km.

④ Turn R, signposted 'Pennine Way Tennant Gill', and run up the grassy track through the fields, past a barn. Continue to follow the path alongside the wall as it bears R, then L to a gate. Pass through the gate, heading for a wall corner. Turn R here and run down the track to a gate. Bear R through the gate and run cross the field to the road. Cross the road and run up the track to **Tennant Gill Farm** 10.2km.

⑤ Follow the track around to the L of the farm, signposted 'Pennine Way'. Run up through the steep field to a wall crossing. Turn R and follow the path for 100 metres. Turn R and follow the path parallel to an old wall up on to

---

Fountains Fell

Fountains Fell gets its name from the Cistercian Fountains Abbey near Ripon, which owned much of the land in the 13th century, including large swathes of the Dales.

The grassy descent into Littondale

Fountains Fell. After about 1km, the path turns R, signposted 'Pennine Way', and traverses along the fell on a gravel path. After another kilometre, cross over a stream, before climbing steeply up to the northern end of **Fountains Fell**. Run across the plateau to a wall crossing, marked by stone cairns at 650m 14km.

(6) Cross the wall and run down the rocky path as it zigzags over a small stream. Follow the path to a wall. Turn R and follow the path to the road. Turn R along the road for half a kilometre to a track 16.3km.

(7) Turn R along the track, following it through **Dawson Close** for a couple of kilometres, contouring above Pen-y-ghent Gill. Continue, to reach a gate above a steep stream gully 18.7km.

(8) Run down the track for 1km, before dropping steeply down into Littondale. Follow the track alongside the river to a bridge. Bear R and run down the walled track to a footpath at **East Garth Farm** 21.8km.

(9) At a barn Turn R, signposted 'Arncliffe', and cross the field, following the path to the riverside. Run along the river and through the fields back to **Arncliffe** 25.5km.

Route 38
Buckden Pike

Start/finish	Limited off-road parking at Starbotton: SD 953 746; alternatively, use the public car park in Buckden Village
Distance	13km (8 miles)
Ascent	555m (1820ft)
Grade	Level 3
Time	2hr
Terrain	A mixture of grassy and stony paths
Map	OS Landranger 98: Wensleydale & Upper Wharfedale
Refreshments	Pubs, toilets and shops in Buckden village
Public transport	Bus 874/875 from Grassington/Hawes

This run takes in a beautiful section of upper Wharfedale, combined with an ascent of one of the Dale's highest peaks.

The run starts with a gentle run up Wharfedale, following a section of the Dales Way, to the picturesque village of Buckden. The next section climbs Buckden Pike, which looms large behind the village, standing out high above the valley. The final section follows the plateau south, before following a good runnable path down into Starbotton.

The Buckden Pike Fell Race

The Buckden Pike Fell Race starts by crossing the small stream, before climbing up the exceptionally steep bank to the right of the car park. More impressive is the speed at which the front-runners descend the bank on their way back to the finish.

---

1 From the road, run along the walled lane, signposted 'Kettlewell' and 'Buckden', to the river Wharfe. Cross the river and turn R alongside the river. Run along a series of paths, walled lanes and tracks, following the **Dales Way** upstream to reach a gate 2km.

2 Continue ahead and then bear L to the woodland. Follow the track along the bottom of the wood. After 800 metres, leave the track and turn R on a small

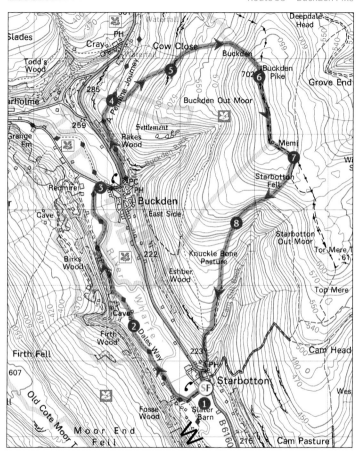

footpath, signposted 'Dales Way', to the riverside. Follow the path alongside the river to reach a road 4km.

3   Turn R along the road to **Buckden**. Turn L alongside the village green and cross into the public car park. Leave the car park through a gate on the L, heading NW to follow a stony track uphill, signposted bridleway 'Buckden Pike'. Follow the track to a junction 5.5km.

4 Take the L fork alongside a wall for 50 metres to another wall. Pass through the gate and turn R, signposted 'Buckden Pike'. Follow the wall first, before the path bears diagonally L. Run uphill through several fields to reach a rocky outcrop. Continue ahead to a wall 6.9km.

5 Run ahead, following a paved path, up a series of steep steps and terraces to the summit of **Buckden Pike** at 702m 8.2km.

6 From the trig point, continue to run along the wall for about 1km to the **Polish war memorial**, at a wall junction. Cross the wall and continue ahead, with the wall on the R, for approximately 400 metres to a path junction and distinctive wall corner 9.3km.

The track leading out of the car park in Buckden

Grassy terraces on the northern slopes of Buckden Pike

7 Turn R through the gate, the start of the descent across **Starbotton Fell**, and follow the stony, cairned path for 200 metres to cross a broken wall. Continue to descend, following a series of blue marker posts, towards the valley. Pass through a gate to reach a junction of broken walls overlooking a V-shaped river valley on the L 10.5km.

8 Run down the grassy path/track, past an old bridleway sign, to a gate. Pass through the gate and follow the rough, stony and steep walled lane into **Starbotton**. Turn L on to the road, then turn R over the river, following the road back to the start 12.9km.

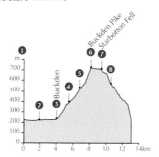

Route 39
Masham Moor

Start/finish	Small riverside car park near Gollinglith Foot: SE 153 809
Distance	19.5km (12 miles)
Ascent	525m (1720ft)
Grade	Level 4
Time	3hr
Terrain	Mainly on large stone tracks with some grassy tracks – two short sections of path require careful navigation
Map	OS Landranger 99: Northallerton & Ripon
Refreshments	Pubs, cafés and shops in Masham
Public transport	Bus 159 to Masham is the closest

This is a straightforward run, along easy-to-follow tracks, through beautiful heather moorland. The best time for this run is late summer or early autumn, when the moors are in covered in purple flowers.

The run has two main sections, with the hardest navigation at the end of each section. The first half climbs through small valleys up on to the moorland plateau, finishing down a small path that leads to a sheep fold high above Nidderdale. The return leg recrosses the moor, finishing with a steep up-and-down section across a wooded valley on a small path, before rejoining the outward route.

Did you know?

Founded by the Anglo Saxons, Masham is home of the Black Sheep Brewery, which provides beers to many of the pubs in the Dales.

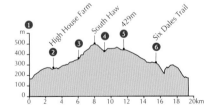

Scar House Reservoir

① From the car park, cross the footbridge. Turn R to the track, then turn L and run up the track past a farm. Continue to run along the track as it rises out of the valley. After nearly 2km, the track descends to a small river gorge. Run along the track to the bridge at **High House Farm** 3.5km.

② Bear L up the track, following the stream, away from the farm and run up the heather-covered valley, crossing a bridge over a stream to a **shooting hut**. Bear R in front of the hut and take the track along the L bank of a small river. The valley narrows and becomes more rugged. Continue along to the river crossing 6km.

Shooting hut at the foot of Masham Moor

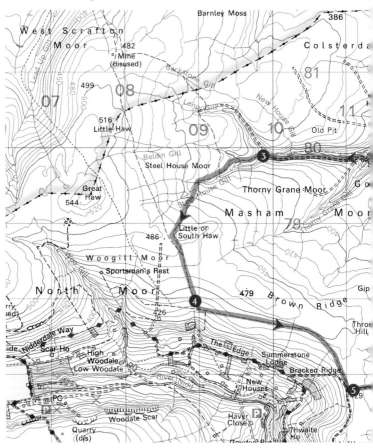

3 Ford the small river and continue uphill for approximately 30 metres to a track junction. Bear L and follow the steep track up over a small shoulder to a second track junction. Bear L and descend to a small stream, before climbing again to the moorland plateau. The track becomes narrower the higher you go. After 1km, descend L over a small stream and run along the rocky, muddy track through the heather moorland to reach a fence and gate beneath **Little or South Haw**. Continue ahead on the small grassy track,

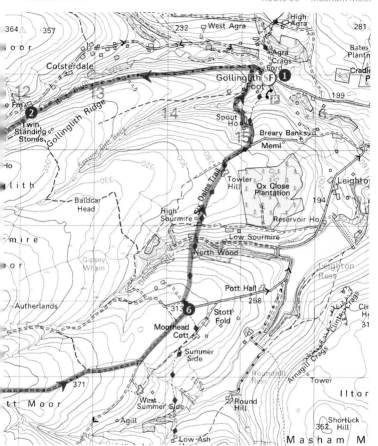

descending slightly. Bear R and follow the very small, occasionally indistinct, path south to a stone sheepfold above a wood 8.9km.

4 Run 100 metres down the small path to the L of the sheepfold, to the track. Turn L along the track and run high above the valley, before descending slightly to a track and wall junction above a patch of woodland at spot height **429m** 11.6km.

Snowy track on the second half of the route

⑤ Pass through the gate. Turn L and run alongside the wall on a grassy track to another gate. Continue ahead on the track across the moor. Run down the track to a junction. Continue ahead to a minor road. Turn L, following the road to a track junction, signposted 'Six Dales Trail' 15.4km.

⑥ Turn L and run down the track to a cattle grid. Bear R through the field on a faint grassy track and descend to a wall junction. Follow the waymarked trail down through the field and into the newly planted woodland. Follow the small path through the wood. Bear R at the bottom and cross the wall into the older wood. Follow the path down to the stream. Cross the stream on a narrow concrete footbridge. Climb up steeply, crossing a track, and run through a small conifer wood. Cross the fields to a ruined farm. Turn R in front of the barn and L at the end of it. Cross two more fields, bearing diagonally R to the end of a line of trees. Cross another wall and field to a ladder stile. Turn L to the farm. Bear L in front of the farm and run down the track to a junction. Turn R and descend to a road and track junction. Turn L and run down the track, through **Spout House Farm**. Follow the track until it rejoins the outward route. Turn R and follow the track back to the start 19.5km.

Route 40
Pendragon Castle to Skipton Castle
Ultra Leg 3 (Kettlewell to Skipton)

Start	Kettlewell public car park and toilets: SD 968 723
Finish	Skipton Castle: SD 99 519
Distance	30.5km (19 miles)
Ascent	730m (2400ft)
Grade	Level 2
Time	4hr 30min
Terrain	Mainly good grassy tracks and paths with sections of stony tracks and road
Map	OS Landranger 98: Wensleydale & Upper Wharfedale
Refreshments	Pubs, cafés and shops in Kettlewell, Grassington and Skipton
Public transport	Bus 874/875 from Grassington/Hawes

This is a straightforward run that passes from the classic limestone country of the central National Park to the gritstone moorlands in the south of the Dales, finishing at the impressive Skipton Castle. The first section runs south from Kettlewell, down the limestone valley of the River Wharfe, to the popular town of Grassington. The second section crosses the valley bottom, via the impressive Linton Falls, and climbs up to the hamlet of Thorpe. The final section crosses the moors of Burnsall and Thorpe Fells, before passing Embsay Reservoir to finish at Skipton Castle.

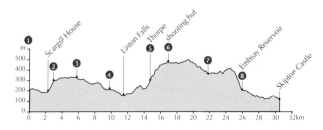

1. Turn L out of the car park and then R along the road, signposted 'Dales Way'. Turn L at the next junction and run ahead, past the Kings Head pub. Turn R at Fold Farm and follow the track through the buildings. Turn L up a grassy walled lane. Follow this to the end. Turn R, signposted 'Dales Way', and run along the footpath through the fields to the road. Turn L and run past **Scargill House** to the track/road junction. Turn L up the track. Run up the track to a gate, continue to climb up the track to a gate at the far edge of the wood 3km.

2. Turn R, signposted 'Grassington', and run alongside the broken wall. Continue to follow the Dales Way along the grassy terrace for a couple of kilometres to a track. Cross the track to a footpath junction and fingerpost 5.7km.

3. Pass through the gates still following the **Dales Way** as it descends gradually through the rough pasture to a lime kiln on the R. Continue ahead to a fork in the path. Bear L through a small section of limestone pavement to reach a footpath junction. Continue ahead for approximately 100 metres to a second junction. Turn R and descend to the fields. Cross the wall and bear L, then R, following the path through the fields to a farm. Continue to follow the path to a track. Turn R and follow the track to the road junction 10km.

Shooting hut on Burnsall Fell

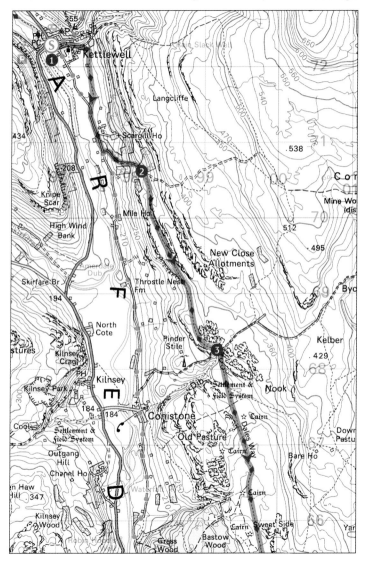

4 Turn L and run down the road to **Grassington** High Street. Turn R and run down to the road junction. Turn L to the National Park Visitor Centre car park. Cross this diagonally (L to the far side). Run down a narrow walled path to **Linton Falls**. Cross the footbridge and follow the path to the road. Turn L alongside the **River Wharfe**. Turn R, signposted 'B6160', up through the fields above the river to the road. Turn R and immediately L. Run up through the terraced grassy fields, signposted 'Thorpe'. Continue into a walled lane. Follow this to the road. Turn L and run along to **Thorpe**. Turn R and descend to the small triangular green 13.9km.

5 Run ahead along the 'No Through Road' towards **Burnsall and Thorpe Fell** to a track junction. Turn L and run up the steep, rocky track to the gate at the top. Bear L and follow the grassy path up a shallow gully to a junction and small cairn. Bear R and follow the path up to a second cairn. Bear L and follow the path up to a track junction and shooting hut 16.2km.

6 Turn R and run along the track, contouring around the moor. After Peter's Crag, the track becomes a path. Follow this along the wall side to the large stone war memorial **obelisk**. Continue to run along the rocky path as it descends, from the moorland summit, to **Rylstone Cross** to meet a track 21.8km.

7 Turn L and run along the track to a junction. Turn sharp R and run past two turf-topped stone buildings. Follow the track down and across the stream, before climbing again over **Embsay Moor**. Turn R at a small pile of stones and follow the track down through Deer Gallows to **Embsay Reservoir**. The track becomes less distinct in places. If in doubt, aim for the R corner of the reservoir. Run along the track to the sailing club 26.5km.

8 Run down the road for a few hundred metres to an old mill pond and race. At the end, turn R over a small bridge down steep steps, signposted 'Brackenley'. Follow the path through the fields and houses to a road. Turn R and then L, following the road down into Hill Top Close. Follow the road to the end and take a small footpath around the back of the houses. Bear L through the field to a road. Cross the road and run down the footpath through the fields to a main road. Turn R and follow the road to a T junction. Turn R and run down to **Skipton Castle** 30.5km.

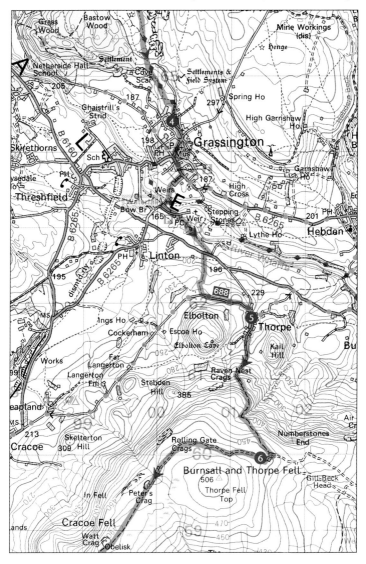

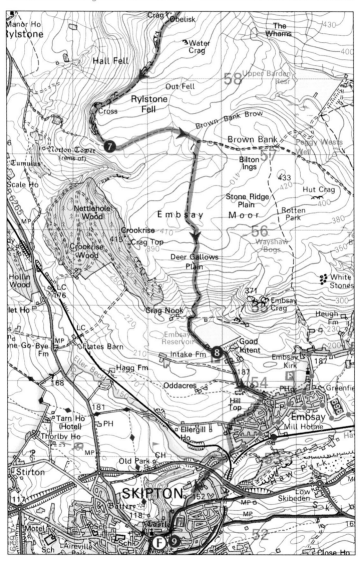

Finishing at Skipton Castle (photo: Adrian Dellbridge)

If you want to keep running

Skipton Castle is the start of Lady Anne's Way, a long-distance route linking Skipton Castle in the south with Broughton Castle (Penrith) in the north.

Appendix A
Useful contacts

Transport

Bus

The Dales Bus
www.dalesbus.org

The Little White Bus
www.littlewhitebus.co.uk

The Northern Dalesman Bus
www.dalesbus.org/northerndalesman

Western Dales Bus
www.westerndalesbus.co.uk

Train

Settle–Carlisle Railway Line
www.settle-carlisle.co.uk

Bentham Railway Line
www.communityraillancashire.co.uk

Trail and fell running resources

British Open Fell Runners Association (BOFRA)
www.bofra.org.uk

Fell Running Association (FRA)
www.fellrunner.org.uk

Long Distance Walkers Association (LDWA)
www.ldwa.org.uk

Trail Running Association (TRA)
www.tra-uk.org

Yorkshire Dales resources

Yorkshire Dales National Park
www.yorkshiredales.org.uk

Yorkshire Tourist Board
www.yorkshire.com

Mountain Weather Information Service (MWIS)
www.mwis.org.uk

The Met Office
www.metoffice.gov.uk

Notes

Notes

Notes

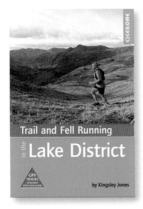

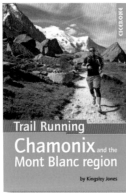
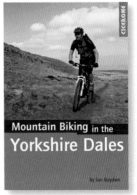

download the routes
in GPX Format

All the routes in this guide are available for download from:

as GPX files. You should be able to load them into most formats of mobile device, whether GPS or smartphone.

When you go to this link, you will be asked for your email address and where you purchased the guide, and have the option to subscribe to the Cicerone e-newsletter.

www.cicerone.co.uk

Listing of Cicerone guides

For full information on all our
guides, books and eBooks,
visit our website:
www.cicerone.co.uk

Walking – Trekking – Mountaineering – Climbing – Cycling

Over 40 years, Cicerone have built up an outstanding collection of over 300 guides, inspiring all sorts of amazing adventures.

Every guide comes from extensive exploration and research by our expert authors, all with a passion for their subjects. They are frequently praised, endorsed and used by clubs, instructors and outdoor organisations.

All our titles can now be bought as **e-books**, **ePubs** and **Kindle** files and we also have an online magazine – **Cicerone Extra** – with features to help cyclists, climbers, walkers and trekkers choose their next adventure, at home or abroad.

Our website shows any **new information** we've had in since a book was published. Please do let us know if you find anything has changed, so that we can publish the latest details. On our **website** you'll also find great ideas and lots of detailed information about what's inside every guide and you can buy **individual routes** from many of them online.

It's easy to keep in touch with what's going on at Cicerone by getting our monthly **free e-newsletter**, which is full of offers, competitions, up-to-date information and topical articles. You can subscribe on our home page and also follow us on **Facebook** and **Twitter** or dip into our **blog**.

Cicerone – the very best guides for exploring the world.

CICERONE

Juniper House, Murley Moss, Oxenholme Road, Kendal, Cumbria LA9 7RL
Tel: 015395 62069 info@cicerone.co.uk
www.cicerone.co.uk